Smart Tax Tips
Winning Strategies to Reduce Your Taxes

More than 145 tax saving tips

Updated for 2002

Grant Thornt

KEY PORTER BOOKS

National Library of Canada Cataloguing in Publication Data

Smart tax tips

Annual.
1998–
"Winning strategies to reduce your . . . taxes".
ISSN 1481-1111
ISBN 1-55263-383-7 (2001 edition)

1. Tax planning–Canada. 2. Income tax–Law and Legislation–Canada. I. Grant Thornton
(Firm)

HJ4661.G77   343.7105'2'05   C98-900795-2

THE CANADA COUNCIL | LE CONSEIL DES ARTS
FOR THE ARTS | DU CANADA
SINCE 1957 | DEPUIS 1957   ONTARIO ARTS COUNCIL
                                           CONSEIL DES ARTS DE L'ONTARIO

The publisher gratefully acknowledges the support of the Canada Council for the Arts and the
Ontario Arts Council for its publishing program.

We acknowledge the financial support of the Government of Canada through the Book
Publishing Industry Development Program (BPIDP) for our publishing activities.

*We've made every effort to ensure the information included in this text is accurate, but no publication should
be used as a substitute for competent professional advice in implementing tax-planning decisions. We invite
our readers to contact any of the Grant Thornton offices across Canada to meet with a tax adviser to discuss
your specific tax situation.*

*Readers should be aware that the commentary in this book is based on the Income Tax Act and all pending
draft legislation and regulations issued by the Department of Finance as of June 30, 2001. Post-publication
changes may have a material effect on the recommendations in this book. Please consult with your tax adviser
to learn of relevant changes to the legislation.*

Key Porter Books Limited
70 The Esplanade
Toronto, Ontario
Canada M5E 1R2

www.keyporter.com

Design: Jack Steiner
Electronic formatting: Jean Lightfoot Peters

Printed and bound in Canada

01 02 03 04 05 6 5 4 3 2 1

A C K N O W L E D G E M E N T S

Smart Tax Tips—Winning Strategies to Reduce Your Taxes has been compiled and written by tax advisers and other professionals from Grant Thornton LLP.

Contributions have been made by the following:
Glen Gilbert—National Service Line Leader, Tax
Karen Yull, National Tax
Jeremy Bast, Kentville
Bill Braun, Hamilton
Jean Byrnes, Hamilton
Gary Dent, Toronto
Connie Dolomount, St. John's
Kristine Douglas, St. Catharines
Scott Elliot, Kelowna
Melissa Gordon, Dartmouth
John Granelli, Winnipeg
John Grummett, St. Catharines
Nora Gubins, National
Marilyn Hayre, Moncton
Renee Higginbotham, Charlottetown
Nandy Heule, National
Bill Kai, Hamilton
Cathy Kuhrt, Toronto
Lucie Laliberté, Montreal
Madelaine Leslie, Kelowna
Susan Mehinagic, Victoria
John Plestid, Mississauga
Craig Scott, Winnipeg
Paul Tsuji, Toronto
Patrick Uzan, Calgary
William Zink, Chicago

You may contact any of the contributors listed above through our Web site at **www.GrantThornton.ca**

Taxes may be a "certain" feature of life, as Benjamin Franklin so famously said, but that doesn't mean they aren't also a changing one. Taxes in Canada appear to be entering a period of fundamental change as governments across the country introduce budgets that propose easing the tax burden on individuals and businesses. The transition period creates some unique opportunities that remind us that effective tax planning is an ongoing activity.

That's why Grant Thornton LLP, a leading Canadian firm of chartered accountants, management consultants, and business advisers, developed *Smart Tax Tips*. This insightful, easy-to-understand book cuts through the clutter and confusion to provide the strength of advice on taxes and Canada's tax rules. This book presents the information you need for your personal or business tax strategies in a quick and easy-to-find manner. Our smart tips will save you time, money, and worry—at tax time and throughout the entire year.

Smart Tax Tips is a product of the wisdom and experience of the tax experts at Grant Thornton LLP. With offices serving communities across Canada, our firm has been helping entrepreneurial people and businesses, public sector managers, and not-for-profit organizations achieve their goals for more than 50 years.

If you are a business owner, corporate manager, employee, budding entrepreneur, home-based business owner, a stay-at-home parent without income, a retiree on a fixed income, or one of the number of Canadians who needs tax help, then *Smart Tax Tips* is for you.

Whatever your situation, whatever questions you might have about eligible deductions, taxes on investments, tax credits, and much more, *Smart Tax Tips* will guide you through. *Smart Tax Tips* has more than 145 practical tips to assist you with your tax-planning strategies and to help you legally minimize the amount of tax you pay.

Smart Tax Tips will help you understand the tax environment in Canada and instill the confidence you need to effectively and intelligently discuss the "how and why" of your tax situation when working with your tax adviser.

Governments typically like to do things in a big way, and the Income Tax Act is no exception. At more than 2,000 pages, it presents a daunting challenge even to those familiar with Canada's tax system.

Few people have hours—let alone days—to pore over the act's contents in search of information pertinent to their circumstances. That's why we designed *Smart Tax Tips* to help you get to the heart of the matter and provide you with sound, useful information. Here's how to get the best out of this publication.

We've formatted the book so that whatever your situation might be, whatever questions you might have, you can retrieve an answer and find appropriate guidance. It is not primarily intended as a beginning-to-end read.

First, there is a comprehensive index that allows you to quickly find the items relevant to your search. It will point you to the one, two, three, or more of the 146 articles that relate to your interest. And remember, when reading the articles, that any discussion of the goods and services tax (GST) also includes the harmonized sales tax (HST) that is in place in Nova Scotia, New Brunswick, and Newfoundland and Labrador.

Second, many of the articles include examples—a sample calculation or perhaps a typical scenario—to help you better understand the way certain rules work.

Third, we feature a **Top 10 Tax Tip List** that highlights some of the more important aspects of strategic tax planning—each one referenced to its appropriate article.

And last but in no way least is this book's reason for being—the tax tips themselves. There are more than 145 tips in this edition. They can help you reduce your taxes in most cases, and also avoid costly tax pitfalls that can arise at times through inadequate tax planning.

We have also included a glossary to help clarify various terms, relevant tax tables, plus a tax calendar to help you plan your 2001 tax return. You will also find a list of Grant Thornton LLP offices throughout Canada, and a form to request up-to-date tax and business advisory information from Grant Thornton via our newsletter, *Cataly$t*.

Of course, with a publication this size, it is virtually impossible to include every tax rule on the books in Canada. What we have attempted to do is to cover the rules that most commonly arise—rules that have implications for most people in everyday business and/or their personal financial situations. However, *Smart Tax Tips* should not be seen as a substitute for competent professional tax advice. Tax planning is a complex process that must be related to your individual circumstances.

What this book can do is give you the familiarity with the tax landscape in Canada to furnish you with an important resource—the knowledge to confidently discuss your tax status with your professional tax adviser.

There is no need to be intimidated when it comes to tax rules. Understanding them is the first step. To that end, we trust that you will find this book exceedingly beneficial. And to keep up with ever-changing tax regulations and rates year-round, visit the Grant Thornton Web site at **www.GrantThornton.ca/tax** and sign up for Smart Tax Tips online. Approximately every two weeks, you'll receive notification by email of the current Smart Tax Tip posted on our Web site.

1. **Maximize your RRSP contributions.** Amounts contributed to your RRSP are deductible from income. As well, tax is deferred on all amounts earned inside your RRSP until you begin receiving an RRSP retirement income (see articles **52** and **53**).

2. **Contribute to your RRSP by December 31 if you turn 69 in the year.** If you turn 69 during 2001, you are required to either convert your RRSP to a RRIF or annuitize your RRSP by December 31. However, you can make a final contribution prior to converting your RRSP. If you have earned income in 2001, in addition to your normal contribution, you could contribute 18% of your earned income. After 69, you can also make contributions to a spousal RRSP if you have earned income and your spouse or common-law partner is not yet 69 (see article **52**).

3. **Make your interest expense tax-deductible.** If you must borrow, try to do so for investment or business purposes before borrowing for personal reasons. The interest paid on these loans is fully deductible; interest on personal borrowing is not (see article **127**).

4. **Split income with your spouse or common-law partner and children.** Most couples will pay less tax overall if each partner earns some of the family's investment income, rather than one partner earning it all (see article **94**). You can also split income with your children by acquiring capital property with a low yield but high capital gains potential in your children's names (see article **91**).

5. **Review plans for charitable donations.** The taxable capital gain on publicly traded securities gifted to a charity up to 2002 is reduced by one-half of the regular rate. To benefit from the reduced inclusion rate, consider donations of qualifying securities instead of cash or other property (see article **75**). If you are planning substantial

bequests, the increase in annual donation limits over recent years may create some tax-planning opportunities (see article **107**).

6. **Claim reserves on sales of capital assets.** If you sell capital assets but the full proceeds of sale are not receivable by year-end, you can bring the taxable portion of the capital gain into income over a five-year period (10 years for small businesses or farm property). However, in structuring the sale, make sure you will have enough to pay the taxes required. If proceeds are deferred over a long period of time, the tax may be due before the proceeds are received (see article **116**).

7. **Realize losses to offset gains.** If you have capital gains in the year and have accrued losses on other investments, consider selling your losers before year-end (see article **117**).

8. **Reduce net income to avoid OAS clawback.** Defer income to a future year or maximize your deductions this year so your net income is reduced and the Old Age Security clawback is minimized (see article **66**).

9. **Use RESPs to assist with education costs.** Consider contributing to an RESP to help finance your child's education. The Canada education savings grant program now makes these plans more attractive than ever (see article **92**).

10. **Take advantage of reduced tax rates.** The federal government and many provincial governments have already announced lower income tax rates for 2002 and beyond. Further tax rate reductions may also be announced as budget surpluses continue to grow. To take advantage of the lowering rates, the receipt of income (such as commissions, bonuses, interest, capital gains) should be deferred wherever possible (see **Table 2**). Log on to the Grant Thornton Web site at **www.GrantThornton.ca/tax** to find the most up-to-date tax tables for federal and provincial tax rates, tax credits, and EI rates.

C O N T E N T S

Businesses

From sole proprietors to owners of multimillion-dollar businesses, every business owner knows that sound tax planning is vital to a healthy bottom line. And every successful business owner also knows that expert professional tax advice is essential to ensure their tax strategies are right on the money.

Understanding how the tax rules work and how they might apply to your particular business circumstances will go a long way toward helping you work more effectively with your tax adviser to develop both short- and long-term approaches to benefit your company.

This section contains a number of tax tips you can apply to improve your tax profile. It also includes 47 pertinent items that address the most common tax situations likely to affect your business's operations. Many of the items pertain to all businesses—whether conducted by the self-employed or carried on through a corporation—whereas others are specific to corporations. It includes information about the various deductions allowed, and also what you need to know about the goods and services and harmonized sales taxes.

As well, this section covers the rules on eligible expenses—what you can deduct and what you cannot, whether it's the cost of business entertainment or operating a vehicle. Other featured areas include depreciation, deferrals, business investment tax credits, inventory issues, business losses, running a home office, and much more.

■ Are you self-employed?

If you are self-employed, you have many more options for tax planning than if you are an employee. Therefore, it makes a lot of economic sense to clearly establish whether you are an employee or self-employed. Determining whether you are self-employed or employed is not always cut and dried—it all depends on your particular circumstances, and it often comes down to how much control the person paying for your services exercises over your work.

For example, if a person (or company) controls your work hours, where you perform the work, and provides all the equipment, supplies, and office help that you need, you are likely an employee. On the other hand, if you provide services to a number of different parties and are in a position to prioritize their demands, you will likely be considered self-employed.

In response to requests from various industry groups, the Canada Customs and Revenue Agency (CCRA) has published a guide to assist in determining employed vs. self-employed status. A copy of this guide (RC4110) can be found on the CCRA's Web site at **www.ccra-adrc.gc.ca** (see Forms and publications—Frequently requested publications).

◳ Your year-end

Not long ago, if you were carrying on a business as a sole proprietor or as a member of a partnership, you (or the partnership) were allowed to establish any fiscal year-end for the business. That meant you were not required to select the December 31 calendar year-end, as all individual employed taxpayers must do. This advantage was eliminated in 1995.

Current rules

Since 1995, all sole proprietors, certain partnerships, and professional corporations that are members of affected partnerships must have a December 31 year-end.

Partnerships affected by this rule include those in which at least one member is an individual, a professional corporation, or another partnership subject to this rule. (A professional corporation is any corporation that carries on the professional practice of an accountant, dentist, lawyer, medical doctor, veterinarian, or chiropractor.)

You may be able to opt out

If you were carrying on business in 1995 or earlier and you had a non-calendar year-end that you wanted to keep, you may be eligible to use an "alternative method" of calculating income for tax purposes. Under this method, your business income was determined using a pro rata formula that adjusted income earned during the fiscal period to a calendar-year basis. However, you should be aware that the pro rata formula might result in greater swings of income from year to year. Because of the way the formula works, the income will often be higher in a good year and lower in a poor year, which can have the negative impact of moving income from a low tax bracket year to a higher tax bracket year.

Eligible taxpayers include individuals and partnerships in which all members are individuals. This election is not available to a partnership that is a member of another partnership.

If you were carrying on business in 1995, you had to make this election when you filed your 1995 tax return. Otherwise, you were required to have a December 31 fiscal year-end. And, once a December 31 fiscal year-end has been adopted, you cannot revert to the alternative method.

If you are starting a new business and would like to employ a non-December 31 year-end, you are strongly urged to contact your tax adviser to determine your eligibility and whether this strategy is of any advantage to you.

Something in reserve

If you were self-employed in 1995 and had to switch to a December 31 year-end, or make adjustments to your non-calendar-year income as though you had a calendar year-end, you may have had to report business income for more than 12 months on your 1995 income tax return.

If this was the case, there was some relief. You were entitled to defer the excess income resulting from the change (i.e., the income from your fiscal period commencing in 1995 to December 31, 1995, or estimate thereof) over a 10-year period by claiming a reserve.

The reserve calculation required a minimum of 5% of this excess income to be included in income in 1995. After that, 10% of that excess is to be included in each of the next eight years (1996–2003), and the remaining 15% will be included in income for the year 2004.

EXAMPLE
Reporting a reserve

Your unincorporated business had a January 31 year-end and earned

$120,000 in the period ended January 31, 1995. Then, from February 1, 1995, to the period ended December 31, 1995, your business earned $100,000.

Assuming you did not elect to retain the January year-end (the "alternative method"), you would have had to report income of $125,000 for 1995, which is $120,000 for the period ended January 31, 1995, and 5% of the $100,000 earned in the period ended December 31, 1995. In each year from 1996 to 2003, income of $10,000 would have to be included. And finally, in 2004, you have to include income of $15,000. The deferral ceases to be available if you do not carry on business at the beginning of the year.

TAX TIP

The amount of reserve claimed each year is optional—provided you include the minimum amount required in income. There may be reasons for including more income in a particular year than the minimum amount required.

TAX TIP

Contemplating a transaction that may affect your status, such as incorporating your sole proprietorship, forming a partnership, leaving one partnership to join another, or retiring? Look before you leap and talk with your tax adviser to review the potential impact your move might have on the deferral.

3 Taxing partnership income

As a member of a partnership, you must report your share of the partnership's profit or loss for the fiscal period ending in 2001. Your 2001 tax return may also have to include income as a result of claiming a reserve in 1995 (see article 2). While you can normally claim your share of partnership losses against your other sources of income, this may not always be the case if you are a member of a limited partnership (see article 129).

The allocation of partnership income or losses is normally left up to the partners to resolve. But, if the tax department determines that the allocation is unreasonable, it may disallow your allocation and substitute what it considers to be a more reasonable one. For example, if you provide the capital and do most of the work in your business, while your spouse contributes significantly less, you can expect the tax department to disallow a 50:50 allocation of the business's income between the two of you.

Expenses that are deductible

Expenses incurred outside the partnership may be deductible. If you borrowed money to invest in the partnership, the interest on that loan is generally deductible. Any expenses that you personally incur in the course of carrying on the partnership business (e.g., promotional and automobile expenses) are also deductible. However, meal and entertainment expenses are only partly deductible (see article 11), and some automobile expenses may be limited (see article 32).

A partnership with more than five partners at any time during its fiscal period is required to file an information return with the CCRA. By the same token, a partnership with fewer than six partners must also file an information return if one of the partners is in another partnership. Each partner must receive an information slip from the partnership, outlining his or her share of partnership income and other items allocated from the partnership.

4 Which province gets your tax?

Employment and investment income are taxed by the province in which you reside on December 31. This holds true even if the income was earned in another province. Business income, on the other hand, is taxed in the province where the business was conducted. If you carry on the same business in more than one province, there is quite an involved formula used to determine what portion of your business income is taxable and in which province. This is best left to your tax adviser's expertise.

EXAMPLE

Income allocation

Generally speaking, business income is allocated to each province based on the pro rata share of the total revenue earned and salaries and wages paid to employees in the province. Assume you have net business income of $100,000. Your head office is in Ontario and there is a sales office in British Columbia. Each office had one employee earning $30,000 per year. Now, if $300,000 in revenue was generated in Ontario and $200,000 was earned in British Columbia, business income would be allocated as follows:

	Revenue ($)	Revenue (%)	Wages ($)	Wages (%)
Ontario	300,000	60	30,000	50
B.C.	200,000	40	30,000	50
Total	500,000	100	60,000	100

Therefore, the business income taxable in Ontario would be $55,000 [100,000 × (60% + 50%) ÷ 2] and $45,000 [100,000 × (40% + 50%) ÷ 2] would be taxable in British Columbia.

TAX TIP

Provincial tax is based on your province of residence at December 31. If you are moving or transferring to a province with a lower tax rate, you should consider accelerating your departure to arrive before the end-of-year deadline. Conversely, if a move to a province with a higher tax rate is in your future, if at all possible postpone your relocation until after the year-end.

5 Paying your spouse or common-law partner and/or children

Salaries paid to your spouse or common-law partner and/or children are tax deductible to your business as long as the wages are reasonable in relation to the services they have provided. As a rule, salaries are considered reasonable if they are representative of an amount that would be paid to an arm's-length party for similar services—in other words, comparable to what you would pay an unrelated employee to do that job.

TAX TIP

There are many advantages to paying reasonable wages to family members for actual services rendered. One is that salaries will be taxed in their hands, and probably at rates lower than the top marginal rate. This arrangement will also allow them to make their own RRSP and CPP contributions.

6 Employment insurance and family members

For family businesses, employment insurance premiums can constitute a considerable expense. There are various exemptions from having to remit EI premiums, however. For example, if you own more than 40% of the voting shares of a corporation, your employment is not subject to EI premiums. There is another exemption for employees who deal at "non-arm's length" with their employer. The problem in this area is that there is another rule that states that two related persons are deemed to deal with each other at arm's length if the circumstances of the employment are substantially similar to what they would be if an unrelated person were to perform the same job. In other words, if an individual not related to you would have been offered the same pay and work arrangements as those provided to your relative for the same services, you generally must withhold premiums from the salary paid to your relative.

TAX TIP

If your spouse or common-law partner or other family members are currently employed by you or your company, review the conditions surrounding their employment to determine if employment insurance premiums are required—you could be eligible for a refund.

7 Calculating depreciation

The cost of a capital asset is generally not deductible as an expense. However, you can depreciate certain business assets for tax purposes. In tax circles, such depreciation is referred to as capital cost allowance (CCA).

Depreciable assets are grouped into classes according to their type and use, and the tax department has come up with more than 40 different classes, each with its own rate of depreciation. Office equipment and furniture, for example, are depreciated at a rate of 20% per annum. General-purpose computers and systems software are depreciated at 30%, as are automobiles (see article 32). Any building acquired after 1987 is usually depreciated at 4%. Most classes of assets are depreciated on a declining-balance basis.

How to calculate

The amount of depreciation you can claim for a year is arrived at by multiplying the remaining balance in the asset class by the percentage rate for that specific class. The remaining balance, referred to as the undepreciated capital cost (UCC), is calculated on a continuous basis.

The general rule is that property may be depreciated for tax purposes at the earlier of either the time it is used to earn income or in the second taxation year following the year of acquisition.

Each year (subject to the available-for-use rules—see below), you add the cost of assets acquired in the year to the previous year's closing balance. If there have been any dispositions, you subtract the sale proceeds, up to the original cost of the disposed assets.

The half-year rule

Most depreciable assets are subject to a rule that reduces the maximum depreciation claim in the year of purchase to one-half of the normal amount. This "half-year" rule does not apply to the acquisition of certain capital property, such as tools costing less than $200 each. You can write them off 100% in the year of purchase.

EXAMPLE

Sample depreciation

Assume that you purchase some equipment in November 2001 for use in your consulting business. Its total cost is $20,000. The equipment would be placed in class 8 and depreciated at a rate of 20% per year subject to the half-year rule. The CCA claim in 2001 and following years would be as follows:

Year	Opening UCC	CCA (20%)	Closing UCC
2001	20,000*	2,000**	18,000
2002	18,000	3,600	14,400
2003	14,400	2,880	11,520

*This is the addition for the year 2001.

**CCA rate for 2001 is 10% (20% × ½)—half-year rule applied in year of purchase.

In computing your business income for 2001, you may claim any amount up to $2,000 in respect of CCA. You may claim a lesser amount if you want, in which case your opening UCC balance for 2002 would be increased accordingly.

Available-for-use rules

The available-for-use rules determine the taxation year in which an amount can first be claimed for depreciation and whether or not the half-year rule will apply. Rules with respect to the acquisition, construction, and/or renovation of a building are especially complex—best to run this by your tax adviser before making a decision.

The maximum depreciation claim may also be reduced for short taxation years. Generally, if the fiscal period of your business is less than 12 months, the depreciation you are entitled to claim is prorated based on the number of days in your fiscal period. However, a few classes of assets are excluded from this rule. Again, it's best to let your tax adviser assess whether or not it applies.

TAX TIP

You should be aware that the rate for a particular class of assets represents the maximum rate that can be applied to the undepreciated capital cost of that class. You do not have to claim the maximum depreciation in any particular year. For example, if your business is in a loss position, you may decide that it is not beneficial to claim depreciation at that particular time.

Special rules and restrictions

Some depreciation restrictions apply to rental property (see articles **108** and **110**) and to depreciation claims arising from certain "tax shelters" where the investor is not active in the day-to-day operation of the business. Depreciation claims by taxpayers who lease certain types of property are also subject to certain rules. Since the rules do not apply to all leasing properties, your tax adviser is in the best position to determine if you are affected by these rules.

In some circumstances, the CCA system does not adequately reflect variations in depreciation actually experienced due to rapid technological change. It is not uncommon at all for some equipment to become obsolete before being fully depreciated for income tax purposes. As a result, a special rule was introduced that allows you to elect to place certain types of capital property into a separate CCA class.

The CCA rate will not change in the separate class. However, if you sell or dispose of the property before five years, you can claim a terminal loss to the extent the UCC of the asset exceeds proceeds from the sale. Eligible property includes the following where each has a cost of $1,000 or more: general purpose electronic data processing equipment, computer software, photocopiers, and certain communications equipment.

8 Amortization and sale of eligible capital property

Eligible capital property can be broadly described as intangible capital property, such as goodwill and other "nothings," the cost of which is neither eligible for capital cost allowance (see article 7) nor deductible in the year of its acquisition as a current expense.

For example, if you purchase goodwill related to a business, you are permitted to depreciate or amortize three-quarters of the cost on a declining-balance basis at the rate of 7%. When the goodwill (the intangible value of a business, such as a recognized name and reputation) is sold, three-quarters of the proceeds are credited to the unamortized pool at the time of sale and, if the balance of the pool becomes negative, the negative balance is taxed as business income. This amount is split between the recapture of amounts previously claimed as amortization and an amount that represents the equivalent of a gain over original cost.

Gains on dispositions of eligible capital property—after recapturing amounts previously deducted—are taxed like capital gains: the amount by which the proceeds exceeds the original cost is taxed at 50% (for taxation years that end after October 17, 2000). At least this is the case where there is only one asset in the cumulative eligible capital (CEC) pool. Where there are other assets in the pool, the rules are more complicated and professional advice is a must.

EXAMPLE

Gain on sale of eligible capital property

Your business has an undeducted balance in its "pool" of $750,000 for the year ended December 31, 2000, and this balance reflects $100,000 of previously claimed amortization. In November, 2001, you dispose of eligible capital property for proceeds of $1,500,000. For the year ended December 31, 2001, your business will report the following:

Opening balance:	$ 750,000
Less: ¾ × $1,500,000	(1,125,000)
Negative balance:	(375,000)
Amount attributable to	
previous amortization	$ 100,000
	(reported as income)
Balance:	$ 275,000
	× ⅔*
Income inclusion	$ 183,333

* 50% × ⅓ (an adjustment to account for the fact that only three-quarters of costs are added to the pool)

There are further adjustments where the taxpayer has an exempt gains balance with respect to the property disposed of (see article **112**).

If the disposition relates to the sale of "qualified farm property," such as an egg or chicken quota, all or a portion of the negative balance may qualify for the capital gains deduction.

TAX TIP

Certain expenditures incurred in relation to a business may not be deductible from income since they are capital in nature but still not eligible for CCA treatment (see article **7**). That being the case, you should review these items with your tax adviser to determine if any of the expenditures would qualify for amortization, as discussed above.

🛚The home office

Many Canadians now work out of their homes, and if you are among this rapidly increasing population you are probably aware that you can deduct a portion of your home office expenses. However, like everything else when it comes to taxation, there are specific rules by which you must abide. Also, the rules are somewhat different depending on whether or not you are self-employed or an employee.

Self-employed

If you are self-employed, expenses must relate to work space that is either your principal place of business or used exclusively for the purpose of earning income from the business. For the second criterion to apply, the space must also be used on a regular and continuous basis for meeting clients, customers, or patients. Space set aside for your business must be a room or rooms used exclusively for the business. Setting up a computer and a filing cabinet in a corner of the living room may not entitle you to claim home office expenses.

Home office expenses can only be deducted from the business carried on in the home and cannot be used to create a business loss. Eligible expenses that you cannot use in the year they are incurred can be carried forward to subsequent years and deducted from income generated by the business at that time.

EXAMPLE

Suppose you started a business in 2001. It generates revenues of $30,000 in 2001 and expenses other than home office expenses of $28,000. The portion of eligible home expenses attributable to your office space amounts to $2,500. In 2001, you will be able to claim only $2,000 of the home office expenses (i.e., $30,000 − 28,000). The remaining $500 of home office expenses can be carried forward and claimed against income generated by the business in the following year, provided there is sufficient income to do so.

TAX TIP

Keep a well-organized file of all receipts and record of payments and go over them with your tax adviser to see if they are eligible deductions for your home business. You may be able to deduct a portion of your house's expenses, such as property taxes, insurance, electricity, heat, and mortgage interest.

TAX TIP

In general, it is not a good idea to claim depreciation on the portion of your home used for business purposes, as there may be tax implications if you ever sell your home. By not claiming depreciation, your entire house may be regarded as your principal residence—that way, any gain realized on the eventual sale of your house may be tax-free.

The GST/HST element

If you are registered for the GST/HST and you qualify to claim home office expenses, input tax credits can be claimed with respect to the portion of your home expenses that is attributable to the business activity. However, an input tax credit can only be claimed for those expenses that are subject to GST/HST—for example, heat, hydro, etc. Mortgage interest, insurance, and property taxes are not subject to the tax. Therefore, no amount can be claimed for these types of expenses.

TAX TIP

If you are a registrant, you can claim an input tax credit for GST/HST paid on home office expenses even if you are not able to deduct them in the year because of the limitation on creating or increasing losses.

EXAMPLE

GST/HST and home office costs

You are a GST/HST registrant, and your only office is located in your home. You regularly meet with clients and conduct all your business from this location. The office space occupies about 20% of the total area of the house. As such, you are entitled to claim a deduction for

20% of the eligible home expenses incurred and input tax credits for 20% of the GST/HST paid on those expenses.

⏸ Paying your dues

Many professionals and business people belong to recreational or dining clubs (e.g., golf and tennis clubs), because, as the old saying goes, "All work and no play . . ." However, annual dues payable to such organizations or facilities are not deductible expenses.

If you pay annual membership dues for an employee, the dues will not be regarded as a taxable benefit to the employee if it can be demonstrated that it is to your advantage for your employee to belong to the club. Similarly, amounts you pay for your employees' use of the facilities for promotional purposes would also not be regarded as a taxable benefit.

What's allowed and what's not

An employee's use of a recreational club for promotional purposes may not be viewed as a taxable benefit. At the same time, the Income Tax Act also specifically denies the employer a deduction for such expenses. The CCRA's position with respect to expenses incurred at a lodge, golf course, or similar facility is as follows: If property such as a lodge or golf course is used for business purposes, and those purposes do not include the entertainment or recreation of clients, suppliers, shareholders, or employees, the department will allow a deduction for the related expenses. For instance, if you hold a business meeting at a golf club and the meeting does not involve playing golf or use of the other recreational facilities, any reasonable expenses incurred will be deductible.

As for meals and beverages consumed at such facilities, deductibility restrictions are the same as for meals and beverages consumed at other establishments (see article 11). You must ensure that the costs are clearly itemized and, of course, incurred for the purpose of earning income. If your records show an all-inclusive charge that does not itemize specific costs, the deduction will not be available.

Keep accurate, timely, and detailed documentation of the business purpose of such expenses to reduce the risk of being denied a legitimate deduction.

Meals and entertainment expenses

There are specific limitations on the amount you can deduct for meals and entertainment. In most cases, only 50% of business meals and entertainment expenses are deductible. And this applies to everyone —individuals, corporations, and partnerships.

A few exceptions

The 50% rule does not apply in certain cases, such as the cost of providing meals consumed and recreation enjoyed by all the employees working at a particular place of business. For expenses incurred after February 23, 1998, this exception applies only to six or fewer special events a year. Meals and entertainment expenses incurred for an event intended primarily to benefit a registered charity also escape the 50% limit. However, the cost of executive dining rooms and similar facilities is subject to the 50% limit. If you attend a convention at which meals and/or entertainment are provided, but the cost of the meals and entertainment is not noted separately, $50 per day will be subject to the 50% rule.

How GST/HST fits in

The ability to claim an input tax credit for meals and entertainment expenses is subject to a similar restriction—only 50% is creditable. You are allowed to claim all the GST/HST paid on such expenses as they are incurred and then make an annual adjustment to add back half of the amount claimed in the year. Alternatively, you may claim only half the GST/HST on such expenses as they are incurred, if this is easier for your accounting purposes.

To simplify the 50% calculation, make a concerted effort to keep such costs segregated from other expenses.

TAX TIP

Meal and entertainment expenses specifically identified on your invoice and billed directly back to your clients are not subject to the 50% limitation. Your client, however, would then be subject to this limitation.

12 Convention expenses

Under current rules, if you are carrying on a business or practising a profession, you can deduct expenses for attending up to two conventions per year. These conventions must relate to your business and be held within the territory in which the sponsoring organization conducts its affairs. You can deduct 50% of the actual cost of meals and entertainment incurred at conventions (see article 11). If you attend a convention at which meals and/or entertainment are provided, but the cost of the meals and entertainment is not noted separately, $50 per day will be subject to the 50% rule.

Expenses must be reasonable and you should be in a position to prove your attendance and to support your expenses with vouchers.

TAX TIP

When your spouse or common-law partner attends a convention with you, the associated cost is usually seen as a non-deductible personal expense. But, if there are good business reasons for him or her to accompany you, these expenses may also be deductible.

13 Canada Pension Plan contributions

Did you earn income from a business as a proprietor or partner in 2001? Then you may be liable for contributions under the Canada Pension Plan (CPP). If you did not earn any employment income in the year, your contribution for 2001 is 8.6% of the difference between your net business income and a $3,500 standard exemption, subject to a maximum contribution of $2,992.80.

If you earned employment income, the amount of CPP premiums that have been withheld from this income is a factor in determining the amount you have to pay. Suppose your 2001 net business income was $30,000. Your CPP contribution for 2001 would be $2,279 [8.6% × ($30,000 − $3,500)]. However, if you also had $10,000 in employment income, your required CPP contributions in respect of your business income would be adjusted to take two factors into account: one, the fact that your total earnings exceed the maximum pensionable earnings ($38,300); and two, the fact that the basic exemption of $3,500 already may have been taken on your employment income. Let's assume you and your employer have already contributed $559 [8.6% × ($10,000 − $3,500)] in respect of your employment income; your CPP contribution in respect of your business income would be $2,433.80 {[(38,300 − $3,500) × 8.6%] − $559}.

Contributions commence the month after you reach the age of 18 and can be made until the age of 70. You can begin to collect CPP benefits as early as age 60 and as late as age 70, depending on when you retire.

Prior to 2001, CPP contributions generated a non-refundable tax credit on your individual tax return. If you are self-employed, the rules have changed somewhat. For 2001 and subsequent years, you can claim a tax deduction for one-half of the CPP contribution that relates to the self-employment income. The remaining one-half continues to qualify for a non-refundable tax credit.

14 Deduction of health/dental insurance premiums

If you are self-employed, you can claim premiums paid for coverage under a private health services plan as a deduction from your business income. But certain limitations apply.

For the premiums to be deductible, you must be actively engaged as a sole proprietor or partner in a business, and self-employment must be either your primary source of income in the current year or your income from other sources must not exceed $10,000.

In addition, equivalent coverage must be extended to all permanent full-time arm's-length employees. Where a deduction is claimed, no amount paid for coverage will be eligible for the medical expense tax credit (see article 77).

If you have no other full-time employees, the deduction is restricted to an annual maximum of $1,500 for each of you, your spouse or common-law partner and other family members 18 years of age or over, and $750 for other members of your household.

15 Deduction of life insurance premiums

If you are required to purchase life insurance as part of the package when borrowing money for business purposes, you can deduct the cost of the premiums, provided certain tests are met. For a deduction to be claimed, the policy must be assigned to the lender as security for the loan and the lender must require this assignment. In addition, the lender's principal business must be the lending of money, and the interest payable on the loan must be deductible for income tax purposes (or would be deductible except in the case of special overriding rules).

The amount that can be claimed is restricted to the lesser of the premium paid and the net cost of pure insurance. The portion of the premium that is deductible could be reduced if the balance of the loan outstanding is less than the amount of insurance coverage.

16 Deduction of fines and penalties

A recent Supreme Court of Canada case allowed a taxpayer to claim an income tax deduction for a levy imposed for violating an egg-producing quota. In this judgement, the court decided that fines, penalties, or levies should be deductible, provided the expense is incurred for the purpose of earning business income (and the deduction is not specifically denied by the Income Tax Act).

Prior to the outcome of this court case, the tax department often disallowed a deduction for judicial and statutory fines or penalties on the basis that to do so would be contrary to public policy. The CCRA recently announced that, in accordance with the principles established by the Supreme Court case, taxpayers will be allowed to deduct fines and penalties incurred to earn income.

Recent tax literature has also suggested that certain penalties imposed under the Excise Tax Act may also be deductible, provided the action giving rise to the penalty was done to earn business income. However, keep in mind that the Income Tax Act specifically prohibits a deduction from income for any interest, penalties, or fines paid under that taxing authority.

If you have been denied a deduction for a fine or penalty incurred in the course of earning income and it is not specifically prohibited by the Income Tax Act, you should contact your tax adviser about requesting an adjustment or filing a notice of objection.

17 Valuation of inventory

Two methods are generally used to establish the value of business inventory for tax purposes. All items may be valued at fair market value (as at the end of the particular year), or each item may be valued at whatever is the lower—its cost or its fair market value.

There are special rules for property that is held as an "adventure or concern in the nature of trade." This designation usually refers to a one-time transaction, often conducted by an individual. Property held as inventory of an adventure in the nature of trade must be valued at the cost at which the taxpayer acquired it, although certain additions to this cost are allowable. What this means is that a loss on such a property cannot be recognized until the property is disposed of. A common example of a situation in which this may apply is if you hold land on the speculation that it can be sold at a profit without further development.

18 Instalment sales

If selling property to your customers on an instalment-sale basis is part of your business, you should be aware of tax rules relating to instalment sales. To qualify for a tax deferral, the instalment sale must be for a period of more than two full years. However, if the property sold was land, the instalment sale need only be for a period that ends after the closing of the fiscal period in which the sale was made.

How much can you defer?

If you qualify, you can spread the profit over a maximum of four years, including the year of sale. The amount you can defer is the pro rata portion of your profit. That is based on the ratio of the amount not due at each year-end, to the total sales price. In the third fiscal year following the sale, you must include all of the remaining untaxed profit in income, even if there is still an amount not due until a subsequent year.

EXAMPLE
Deferring tax

An airplane manufacturer sells a number of planes to a customer on March 31, 2001, for $1,200,000 and realizes a gross profit of $300,000 on the sale. Terms of the sale require $400,000 to be paid on delivery and another $400,000 on June 30, 2002, and June 30, 2003. Assuming a December 31 year-end, the amount of profit available for the deferral in each year is calculated as follows:

2001: $(800,000 \div \$1,200,000) \times \$300,000 =$ $\$200,000$
2002: $(\$400,000 \div \$1,200,000) \times \$300,000 =$ $\$100,000$
2003: $(\$0 \div \$1,200,000) \times \$300,000 \qquad =$ $\$ \quad 0$

As a result of the deferral, the gross profit of $300,000 will be included in income as follows:

2001: $100,000
2002: $100,000
2003: $100,000

A different set of rules applies to instalment sales of property taxed as capital gains (see article **116**).

19 Operating losses and prior years' taxes

If you carried on a business as a proprietor or partner in 2001 and incurred an operating loss, you can apply the loss against other sources of income, such as investment income, capital gains, and employment income. Losses on certain farming businesses may be restricted for the year. If your losses relate to farming activity, check with your tax adviser to determine how much you can claim.

How it works

Any loss realized in a year must be deducted in full against your other sources of income. As a result, you may find that you are unable to claim some or all of your non-refundable tax credits, such as personal amounts and medical expenses. To that end, you should check with your tax adviser to assess whether other family members can obtain the maximum benefit from these lost credits.

Should your operating loss exceed your other sources of income, the excess may be carried back three years or forward up to seven years. To carry the loss back, you must file form T1A with your return for the year in which the loss arises. Technically, you are supposed to make the request by the filing deadline for the year the loss arises. However, the tax department tends to use its discretion as long as the prior year is still open to reassessment. You are free to choose the year to which you want to apply the loss. For example, if you expect your marginal rate of tax to increase in the future, you may decide to carry the loss forward rather than back to a prior year.

TAX TIP

When carrying a loss back to a prior year, you have the option of using only a portion of your loss. For example, you might only want to claim the loss against income that was taxed at a higher marginal rate, and apply the remaining unusable loss to another year.

20 To incorporate or not

Should you consider the possibility of transferring your business to a corporation? It depends on your circumstances and the amount of income you earn. If you are currently carrying on a business as a proprietor or in a partnership, it's worth considering incorporation. As a first step, you should talk it over with your tax adviser, who can "crunch the numbers" and examine the advantages and disadvantages of being incorporated.

Business income earned as a proprietor or partner is subject to income tax at your personal marginal rates. In successful years, you must pay proportionately more income tax, as the extra income places you in a higher tax bracket. However, if you can conduct your business within a corporation, income that qualifies for the small business deduction (see article 22) is taxed at a relatively low rate.

If you incorporate your business and can retain earnings in the corporation for growth, you will be able to defer tax to the extent the earnings are not distributed to you as a salary or dividend (see article 24).

As an added benefit, with appropriate planning, shares of a small business corporation may be able to qualify for the enhanced $500,000 capital gains deduction on their disposition (see article 112).

Incorporate tax-free

Most business assets can be transferred to a corporation without incurring income taxes on the transfer. But there are some rules that apply, which means you must follow definite procedures and meet specific criteria. Your tax adviser can advise you on the merits of incorporation and how it might be accomplished on a tax-deferred basis.

Also, you must remember to consider the impact of incorporation on the deferral claimed for 1995 business income (see article 2). At the same time, you will have to address GST/HST considerations (see article 45), property transfer tax, retail sales tax, and other non-tax issues.

21 Integration

The concept of integration is critical to the proper operation of our tax system and ensures that you won't incur double taxation when you earn income in a corporation—once when it is taxed in the company, and again when you take the earnings out of the company as either a salary or dividend.

According to this concept, income that is distributed to you through a corporation as either salary or a dividend should attract about the same amount of tax as if you had earned it directly. Because actual corporate and personal tax rates differ from what would achieve perfect integration, integration is never exact; the differences will depend on the type of income, your province of residence, and the province in which the company carries on business.

Your particular circumstances will determine whether earning income directly or through a corporation is preferable. Active business income earned by a corporation, taxed at the small business rate and distributed as a dividend, will usually attract less total tax than direct income. On the other hand, income taxed at the top corporate rate and subsequently paid out to you could result in double taxation— particularly if you are in the top tax bracket. That's why it's often recommended to bonus down to the small business limit (see article 22).

22 The small business deduction

Canadian-controlled private corporations (CCPCs) are entitled to claim a small business deduction on active business income earned in Canada. The definition of "active income" is generally intended to exclude corporations created to earn what would otherwise be considered investment or employment income of the individual shareholder. Rates vary from province to province, but this deduction produces a combined tax rate that is anywhere from 15% to 27% lower than the general rate. The lowest rate applies to annual income up to $200,000 and is shared by an associated group of companies (see article 23).

Restrictions do apply

For any tax year ending after June 30, 1994, larger corporations will find that their ability to claim the small business deduction is restricted. The restriction applies to CCPCs whose taxable capital—generally equal to a company's retained earnings, share capital, and long-term debt—exceeds $10 million for the preceding year. If the taxable capital is between $10 million and $15 million, the amount eligible for the low rate is proportionately reduced. Any eligibility ceases if taxable capital surpasses $15 million.

Special rules apply to corporations that are associated for income tax purposes with other corporations (see article 23).

Additional reduction in corporate tax rate

The federal rate of tax (before surtax) on income that qualifies for the small business deduction is 12%—16% lower than the general corporate rate of 28%. Those corporations that are eligible to claim the small business deduction also benefit from an additional 7% reduction in the federal tax rate—to 21%—on Canadian active business income between $200,000 and $300,000. As with the $200,000 small business limit, this additional $100,000 is shared by an associated group of companies.

For other corporations not currently eligible for preferential corporate tax treatment, the general corporate rate of 28% will be reduced to 21% by January 1, 2004. This reduction does not apply to corporations

that are not CCPCs, investment corporations, mortgage investment corporations, mutual fund corporations, or non-resident-owned investment
corporations.

This 7% reduction will be phased in as follows:

January 1, 2001	1%
January 1, 2002	3%
January 1, 2003	5%
January 1, 2004	7%

EXAMPLE

Lower tax rate

Suppose a CCPC earning income from an active business carried on in
Canada has taxable income of $400,000 for its fiscal period ended
December 31, 2001. The income eligible for the small business
deduction (i.e., up to $200,000) will be taxed at the lowest federal tax
rate of 12%. The next $100,000 will be taxed at the reduced 21% tax
rate, and the remaining $100,000 will be taxed at a rate of 27%. The
corporate surtax of 4% continues to be based on the general corporate rate of 28%.

23 Associated company rules

To prevent taxpayers from creating more than one corporation to enjoy
the benefits of the small business deduction, the tax department requires
that the annual limit of $200,000 be shared among associated companies.
The application of the concept of associated companies is a common one
in the Income Tax Act, and the definition, like that of many other tax
rules, is quite complex. The simplest cases are those where companies are
under common control or where one is controlled by the other.

EXAMPLE

ABCs of association

Company A controls Company B, so Company A and Company B are
associated with each other. If Company A also controls Company C,
then each of companies A, B, and C are associated with each other.

Control of a company is not just measured by ownership of the voting shares. In addition to the traditional voting control test, "control" is recognized if a person, or group of persons, owns more than 50% of the fair market value of all of the issued shares, or more than 50% of the corporation's common equity shares. Control can also arise when a person, or group of persons, has any direct or indirect influence that, if exercised, would result in control "in fact" of the corporation.

Sorting out ownership

Who owns the shares? The tax department looks through a corporation to deem the ownership in the hands of the shareholders of a corporation. For example, if you own 60% of one company, which in turn owns 30% of another company, you are regarded as owning 18% (60% of 30%) of the company that is owned by your company.

Shares owned by children under 18 are generally considered to be owned by the parent. In addition to all the technical rules governing association, a general rule is still on the books whereby companies are considered to be associated if one of the main reasons for their separate existence is to save tax.

The concept of control is quite far reaching, yet it is possible for related persons to invest in each other's companies and still remain unassociated. To accomplish that, the cross-ownership has to be less than 25%. As a case in point, if you own 100% of Company A and 20% of Company B, with the other 80% owned by your spouse, Company A and Company B will not automatically be associated. However, if you own 25% or more of Company B, the two companies will be associated. Also, certain types of shares known as shares of a "specified class" are specifically excluded in determining control and cross-ownership.

TAX TIP

Do you have an interest in one or more companies that are related to each other or to other companies? If so, have your tax adviser review the corporate structure to see whether you are deemed to be associated and if there are ways to prevent association.

24 Salary versus dividends

Once your business is incorporated, you must remember that the corporation's profits are not yours to take. The corporation is a separate legal
entity. To extract funds, you must either receive a dividend from the corporation or have it pay you a salary. In addition, if you have loaned money
to your company, you can arrange to receive interest on the loan.

Several rules of thumb help determine the best amount to be paid as
salary, which is deductible to your corporation, and the amount to be
taxed in the corporation and subsequently distributed as a dividend.
Careful analysis is needed to calculate the best mix of salary, interest,
and/or dividends for your specific circumstances.

EXAMPLE

Pay less tax

Using 2001 tax rates, if you earn business income as a sole proprietor
that is taxed at the top marginal rate in Ontario, you will pay 46.41%
in tax. However, the same income earned by your corporation, taxed
at the small business rate and distributed to you in the form of a dividend, will be subject to a combined tax of approximately 45%. These
results will vary, depending on the province in which you reside and
conduct your business.

TAX TIP

If your mix of salary and dividends changes from year to year, it can affect
your tax instalment requirements. Ensure that you and your corporation
are remitting the appropriate amounts.

TAX TIP

Consider paying yourself enough salary to make maximum CPP and
RRSP contributions.

25 Deferred salaries

Rules relating to unpaid salaries have become quite complex. For the
most part, they are intended to match the timing of the employer's

deduction for paying the salary with the employee's reporting of income. For example, if at the end of 2001 an employee is entitled to receive an amount in a future year, and one of the main purposes for this arrangement is to defer or postpone taxation, the amount will be taxed as a benefit to the employee in 2001. This is referred to as a "salary deferral arrangement."

Exclusions

Some plans are excluded from this classification—arrangements to fund certain employee leaves of absence, for example. The rules also do not apply to bonuses paid within three years following the end of the year in which the amount became payable. However, if the bonus is not paid within 179 days from the end of the employer's taxation year, the employer will not be able to deduct the amount until the year it is paid.

TAX TIP

If your corporation's year-end comes after July 6, it can deduct the bonus in the current year and the employee does not have to report the amount as income until the next year. However, the corporation must declare the bonus as of its year-end, and not pay it out until after December 31. Again, the bonus must be paid within 179 days of the year-end to be deductible.

26 Directors' fees

In addition to being an employee of your own company, you—and your spouse or common-law partner and other family members—can also be directors. Directors' fees are considered to be employment income and also constitute earned income for determining how much you can contribute to a RRSP (see articles **52** and **53**).

TAX TIP

If your spouse or common-law partner is a director of your corporation, consider paying a director's fee for services performed. Such services usually include attending directors' meetings, directing the management and affairs of the business, approving financial statements, declaring dividends, etc. On the downside, directors are jointly liable with all other directors for the fulfillment of certain regulatory requirements, such as payroll and GST/HST remittances (see article **145**).

27 Loans from your corporation

As mentioned in article 24, you can withdraw funds from your company by paying yourself either a salary or a dividend. You can also access funds via a loan. The rules in this area are quite complex. Before borrowing funds from your company, you should thoroughly discuss this strategy with your tax adviser to be sure you don't violate certain tax rules.

Repayment timing critical

In general, loans that are not repaid within one year from the end of the year in which they were made will have to be reported as income for the year the loan was made. For example, if you borrow $10,000 from your company on June 1, 2001, and your company has a September 30 year-end, you must report the $10,000 as income on your personal income tax return for the 2001 taxation year if the loan remains unpaid on September 30, 2002.

Some exceptions apply

Shareholders who are also employees can be exempted from the above rules. However, only some types of loans qualify, such as a loan that enables you to acquire treasury stock in your company (or a related company) or finance an automobile to be used in performing your employment duties. A loan to enable you or your spouse or common-law partner to purchase a home may also qualify. However, the rules in this area are complex and professional advice is recommended. To qualify for one of these exceptions, bona fide arrangements must be made, at the time the loan is taken out, to repay it within a reasonable period.

Also, to qualify for the exception from the general rule, loans made after April 26, 1995, must be attributable to your position as an employee and not because of your shareholder status. To determine if it is reasonable to conclude that you received the loan because of your employment rather than your share ownership, you must be able to show that a similar loan would be made to employees who were not shareholders of the company. This might be difficult in the case of a low-interest or non-interest-bearing housing loan, particularly where your company only employs family members.

There is another exception from these rules if lending money is part of your company's ordinary business. Again, you must make bona fide arrangements to repay the loan at the time the money is borrowed.

One more exception

As a relieving provision, an exception to the general rule covers loans made to an employee who is not a "specified employee," provided bona fide arrangements are made when the funds are borrowed to repay the debt within a reasonable time period. A specified employee is generally a shareholder who owns 10% or more of any class of shares of the employer corporation or who does not deal at arm's length with the employer corporation. But be forewarned that if anyone related to you holds shares in the company, the CCRA will deem you to be the owner of these shares for purposes of assessing the 10% rule.

Deemed interest benefit on "excepted" loans

If the loan qualifies for one of the exceptions, this only means that the amount borrowed does not have to be included in your income. However, you will still have to report a taxable benefit based on a prescribed rate of interest that is adjusted quarterly. These rules also apply to most loans to employees (see article **30**).

Using the loan to acquire eligible investments or to earn income, as opposed to using the funds for personal purposes, allows you to claim the amount of the taxable benefit as a deductible interest expense.

TAX TIP

Did you receive a low-interest or interest-free loan from your company? And did you use the proceeds for a qualifying investment? Then make sure you claim the deemed interest deduction.

28 Corporate losses and change of control

When you acquire control of a corporation, a number of rules restrict your ability to carry forward losses incurred before your takeover. At the same time, some of these rules require certain adjustments to various accounts for income tax purposes. The intent is to crystallize any losses inherent in the corporation's assets.

Claiming losses

Claiming non-capital (operating) losses in any period after the change of control requires the business that generated the losses to be carried on throughout the year with a reasonable expectation of profit. In addition, these losses may only be claimed to the extent of the income generated from that business or a similar business. Similar rules apply on the carry-forward of unused scientific research and experimental development (SR&ED) expenses and business investment tax credits. Any unused net capital losses at the time of the change in control may not be used after that point.

TAX TIP

There are some tax-planning techniques available to utilize operating losses that might otherwise be forfeited in the carry-forward period. If you are considering acquiring control of a corporation in an effort to utilize its tax losses, SR&ED expenses (see article **35**), or investment tax credits (ITCs) (see article **35** in part), make sure you are fully aware of the rules as they apply to your situation before you make your purchase.

29 Taxable benefits

If you provide your employees with benefits in addition to their regular salary, an amount must generally be included in their income as a taxable benefit. The most common taxable benefits are company cars (see article **31**), employee loans (see article **30**), and stock options (see article **34**).

In addition, the following less obvious benefits may also have to be included in your employees' income:

Christmas parties and other special events

A recent tax court decision determined that an employee was required to report a taxable benefit with respect to the "benefit" he realized from attending his company's Christmas party. The tax department has since set out guidelines on how it intends to apply the taxable benefit provision to employer-provided social events such as Christmas parties.

In general, no taxable benefit will have to be reported for social events that are made available to all employees, provided the cost per employee is $100 or less. Parties costing more than that will generally be considered to be beyond the "privilege" point and may result in taxable benefits.

Employer-paid professional membership fees

A few years ago, the tax department reconsidered its position on employer-paid professional membership fees and made a ruling effective for 1997 and subsequent years.

In general, the payment of a professional membership fee will not be considered a taxable benefit if the employer is the primary beneficiary of the payment. The employer will be considered the primary beneficiary where membership in the association is a requirement of employment. Where membership is not a condition of employment, the question of primary beneficiary must still be resolved. The employer is responsible for making this determination and may have to report a taxable benefit for the amount paid on employees' behalf.

30 Employee loans

In general, if you provide an employee with a loan at little or no interest, he or she must report a taxable benefit computed as the interest on the loan at a prescribed rate, less any interest actually paid on the loan within the year or 30 days after year-end.

Special rules apply where you provide your employees with a low-interest or interest-free loan to assist them in buying a home in order to begin work at a new location. The taxable benefit arising from this arrangement may be partially or entirely offset by a special deduction.

To qualify, the new residence must be at least 40 kilometres closer to the new work location than the old residence. In general, this special deduction will entirely offset the taxable benefit arising from low-interest or interest-free loans of $25,000 or less. This deduction applies for a five-year period commencing on the date the loan is made.

Special rules also apply if you provide any of your employees with a "home purchase loan," and it is not necessary for the employee to move to a new work location to qualify under this rule. The borrowed money only has to be used to either purchase or refinance the debt on the employee's home. The benefit from such loans is computed by applying either the prescribed rate at the time the loan is granted or the prescribed rate for the particular quarter, whichever is lower. A new base rate on the loan will be established every five years.

Not all benefits have to be included in your employees' income. Certain fringe benefits can still be received by an employee tax-free—for example, employer contributions to registered pension and deferred profit sharing plans (within limits), tuition fees for courses taken for the employer's benefit, employee counselling services paid for by the employer, etc. Your professional adviser can assist you in devising a tax-effective remuneration strategy for your employees.

31 Personal use of a company-owned automobile

If you provide any of your employees with a vehicle for their personal use, a taxable benefit has to be reported. This benefit is comprised of two parts: a "standby charge," which reflects the personal access to the car, and an operating benefit, which reflects the personal portion of operating expenses paid by your company.

In general, the standby charge is 2% of the original cost of the car, including PST and GST (or HST), for each month in the year the car is made available for use. If the car is leased, the standby charge is two-thirds of the lease cost including PST and GST (or HST), net of insurance costs.

The standby charge can be reduced if the vehicle is used 90% or more for employment purposes. Accurate mileage records to support this claim should be maintained. In general, travel between a taxpayer's regular work location and home is considered personal.

The standby charge is calculated on the original cost of the car and does not decrease as the car's value declines with age. After a few years, it may be advantageous to eliminate this benefit by having the employee buy the car from the company at its fair market value.

Employees who sell or lease automobiles may qualify for a reduced standby charge. In these cases, the standby charge is generally computed at 1.5% instead of 2%.

Operating cost

For 2001, the "operating cost" benefit is calculated as 16¢ per kilometre for personal use, less amounts reimbursed to the company in respect of the operating costs. This amount includes a GST/HST component.

If the automobile is used primarily (more than 50%) for employment purposes, there is an optional formula that can be used to determine the operating cost benefit. It can be calculated as 50% of the standby charge.

If your company is a GST/HST registrant, the taxable benefit is deemed to be a taxable supply and GST/HST must be remitted on the benefit amount (see article **43**).

32 Automobile expenses

Rather than providing your employees with a vehicle, it is often more tax-effective for them to acquire the vehicle personally. If it is used for business purposes, a deduction might be claimable for automobile expenses.

The rules governing automobile deductions are extremely complex and cannot be covered here in any great detail. They apply equally to corporations, proprietors, and partnerships, as well as to employees who qualify to claim automobile expenses against their employment income.

Expenses must first be split into two categories—those that are subject to specific dollar limitations and those that are not. Depreciation, interest, and leasing charges are subject to specific dollar restrictions. In general, the amount you can claim with respect to these expenses depends on when the vehicle was acquired. Here are the maximum amounts relating to when the vehicles were purchased:

	Depreciation base	Monthly interest
After August 1989 and before 1991	$24,000 (including PST)	$300
1991 to 1996	$24,000 (plus PST & GST or HST)*	$300
During 1997	$25,000 (plus PST & GST or HST)*	$250
1998 and 1999	$26,000 (plus PST & GST or HST)*	$250
During 2000	$27,000 (plus PST & GST or HST)*	$250
After 2000	$30,000 (plus PST & GST or HST)*	$300

* GST/HST is not included in the depreciation base if it is refunded as an input tax credit

The maximum amounts for vehicle leases are as follows:

	Monthly lease payment
Leases entered into after **August 1989 and before 1991**	$650 (including PST)
Leases entered into from **1991 to 1996**	$650 (plus PST & GST or HST)
Leases entered into in 1997	$550 (plus PST & GST or HST)
Leases entered into in 1998 and **1999**	$650 (plus PST & GST or HST)
Leases entered into in 2000	$700 (plus PST & GST or HST)
Leases entered into after 2000	$800 (plus PST & GST or HST)

For unincorporated businesses and employees, the total of the restricted and unrestricted expenses is then prorated between business and personal use based on the number of kilometres driven for each purpose. Expenses such as parking incurred entirely for business purposes can be claimed in full. Corporations do not have to prorate expenses between business and personal use. Expenses can be claimed in full, provided they are reasonable. However, the employee benefit rules may require a benefit to be included in the employee's income. Also, the employee benefit (standby charge) is calculated based on the actual cost of the vehicle rather than the above reduced amounts (see article **31**).

If a proprietor or partner uses a vehicle less than 100% for business purposes, the eligible depreciation claim for the year is generally determined by the percentage of business use.

TAX TIP

Detailed records should be kept regarding a vehicle's business and personal use. These records must be accurately maintained to support the percentage claimed for business use if the tax department ever calls it into question. Keep in mind that it is the CCRA's position that travel between a taxpayer's regular work location and home is considered personal.

33 Tax-free travel allowances

You can eliminate a lot of the paperwork for your employees by providing them with a tax-free allowance to cover employment-related travel expenses.

The allowance qualifies for **tax-free status** if it is reasonable—and only if it is based on the actual number of kilometres that the car is used for employment purposes. Provided the per-kilometre reimbursement is reasonable, 100% of the amounts paid are deductible.

Allowances that are not based upon the number of kilometres driven, such as a flat allowance of $400 per month, must be included in the employee's income. You can reimburse an employee for certain limited expenses—supplementary business insurance, parking costs incurred for business purposes, toll and ferry charges—without affecting the tax-free status of the allowance, provided the per-kilometre requirement is met.

The CCRA has recently changed its position with respect to employees who receive a combination of flat-rate and per-kilometre allowances. Previously, if you paid your employee such a combination allowance—for example, $200 per month plus 25¢ per kilometre—only the flat-rate portion had to be included in the employee's income. Starting January 1, 2001, both components of such allowances will have to be included in the employee's income and payroll deductions should be modified accordingly.

TAX TIP

If you currently pay any of your employees a combination flat-rate and per-kilometre allowance, consider changing the entire allowance to a per-kilometre reimbursement.

TAX TIP

If the employment portion of travel expenses exceeds the amount of the tax-free allowance, the employee may be able to include the allowance in income and claim related expenses. To do this, the allowance must be considered unreasonable. Since this treatment has been the subject of some recent court cases, professional advice may be required.

As with almost everything else, travel allowances also have GST/HST implications—to both the employer and the employee. The treatment varies, depending on whether the payment is taxable or not taxable to the employee (see article 43).

34 The score on stock options

As an incentive strategy, you may provide your employees with the right to acquire shares in your company at a stated price for a stated period of time. Normally, the shares will be worth more than the purchase price at the time the employee exercises the option.

For example, you provide one of your key employees with the option to buy 1,000 shares in the company at $5 each. This is the estimated fair market value per share at the time the option is granted. When the stock price rises to $10, your employee exercises his option to buy the shares for $5,000. Since their current value is $10,000, he has a profit of $5,000.

How is the benefit taxed?

The income tax consequences of exercising the option depends on whether the company granting the option is a Canadian-controlled private corporation (CCPC), the period of time the employee holds the shares before eventually selling them, and whether the employee deals at arm's length with the corporation.

If the company is a CCPC, there will not be any income tax consequences until the employee disposes of the shares, provided the employee is not related to the controlling shareholders of the company. In general, the difference between the fair market value of the shares at the time the option was exercised and the option price—i.e., $5 per share in the above example—will be taxed as employment income in the year the shares are sold. The employee can claim a deduction equal to one-half of this amount (one-quarter for dispositions before February 28, 2000, and one-third for dispositions after February 27, 2000, and before October 18, 2000) if certain conditions are met.

One-half of the difference between the ultimate sale price and the fair market value of the shares at the date the option was exercised will be reported as a taxable capital gain or allowable capital loss (this income inclusion rate was three-quarters if the property was disposed of before February 28, 2000, and two-thirds for dispositions after February 27, 2000, and before October 18, 2000—see article 111). The portion that is taxed as a capital gain may be eligible for the $500,000 capital gains deduction for shares of a qualified small business corporation (see article 113).

EXAMPLE
_____

Cashing in on stock options

In 2000, your company (a CCPC) offered several of its senior employees an option to buy 1,000 shares at $1 each. In 2001, the company performs very well and the value of the stock doubles. Several of the employees decide to exercise their option. By 2003, the value of the stock has doubled again—to $4 per share—and some of the employees decide to sell their shares. Since the company was a CCPC at the time the option was granted, there is no taxable benefit until the shares are sold in 2003. The benefit is calculated as follows:

Employment income:	
Employment income ($2 − $1) × (1,000 shares)	$1,000
Income deduction (50%)	(500)
Income inclusion	$ 500
Capital Gain:	
Proceeds of disposition ($4 × 1,000 shares)	$4,000
Cost base ($2 × 1,000 shares)	(2,000)
Capital Gain	2,000
	50%
Taxable Capital Gain	$1,000

In the above example, what would happen if the share value declines to $1 per share at the time of sale in 2003? In this case, the employee would report a $1,000 capital loss ($500 allowable capital loss). Unfortunately, while the taxable benefit in 2001 was afforded the same tax treatment as a capital gain, it was not considered a capital gain but employment income. And because the stock option taxable benefit was not a capital gain, the capital loss realized in 2003 cannot be carried back to offset the income inclusion in 2001.

Different treatment for public companies

If the company granting the option is a public company, or not a CCPC, the rules are somewhat different. If such an option was exercised prior to February 28, 2000, the difference between the fair market value of the shares at the time the option was exercised and the option price was taxable as employment income in the year the option was exercised. If certain conditions were met, the employee could claim one-quarter of this taxable benefit as a deduction from employment income. This treatment often forced the employee to sell some of the shares to pay the resulting tax bill.

Recognizing that stock options have become an increasingly important incentive for recruiting and retaining key employees, new rules have been introduced to provide eligible employees with tax treatment similar to employees of private companies, who generally do not have to pay tax until they actually sell their shares. This deferral is effective for options exercised after February 27, 2000, and is subject to a $100,000 annual vesting limit. This limit is based on the fair market value of the underlying shares at the time the option is granted to the employee.

In general, "eligible employees" must deal at arm's length with their employer and any related corporation, and they cannot own 10% or more of the shares of any class of the corporation or any related corporation. In addition, the amount paid by the employee to acquire the security cannot be less than the fair market value of the security at the time the option was granted.

Employees who wish to defer taxation of a stock option benefit must file an election with either their employer or the person responsible for filing their T4 information slip. For qualifying shares acquired in 2000, this election had to be filed no later than August 13, 2001. For 2001 and subsequent years, the deadline will be January 15 of the year following the year in which the options are exercised.

This election is to take the form of a letter containing the following information:

- a request to take advantage of the deferral;
- the amount of the deferral;
- confirmation that the taxpayer was a resident of Canada when the shares were acquired; and
- confirmation that the annual $100,000 limit has not been exceeded.

The onus is on the employee and not the employer to make the election, and the election allows the employer to reduce income tax withholding by the amount of tax attached to the benefit being deferred. However, the stock option benefit—deferred or otherwise—must still be reported on the employees' T4 slips for the year the option is exercised. Employees then file a special form with their tax return (form T1212— Statement of Deferred Stock Option Benefits) that keeps track of the stock option benefits deferred. This form must be filed for each year there is a balance of deferred stock option benefits outstanding.

To the extent a public company employee does not qualify for the above deferral, the old rules continue to apply—i.e., the difference between the fair market value of the shares at the time the option is exercised and the option price will be taxable as employment income in the year the option is exercised. When certain conditions are met, a deduction equal to one-half of the taxable benefit is allowed.

TAX TIP

Consider option arrangements that allow employees to receive a cash payment equal to the value of the options in lieu of shares. Where the plan gives the employee the choice, the same tax consequences apply to the cash payment as would apply to the issuance of the shares—the employment benefit is included in income and the related 50% deduction is available if certain conditions are met. However, the employer may be able to deduct 100% of the cash payment from taxable income.

Options held at the date of death

Special rules come into play when an employee holds unexercised options under an employee stock option plan on the date of death. In general, the difference between the fair market value of options held immediately before death and the price paid to acquire the options is reported as employment income on the taxpayer's final income tax return (subject to a 50% deduction if certain conditions are met). If the stock option is exercised or otherwise disposed of within the first taxation year of the estate, the legal representative can elect to treat any decline in value— from the date of death to the date of exercise or sale—as a loss from employment for the year in which the taxpayer died.

35 Qualified scientific research expenditures

Writeoffs and tax credits above and beyond your usual business deductions are possible if you conduct scientific research that relates to your business. Scientific research and experimental development (SR&ED) consists of pure research, applied research, and experimental development. Of these three activities, experimental development is often the most difficult to evaluate. Part of the problem is that it is often difficult to define what constitutes "development." It is also equally difficult to distinguish exactly when development ceases and production begins—and production does not qualify as research and development. Your accountant will be able to assess if your SR&ED qualifies or what you may have to do to ensure it is recognized by the CCRA.

What can you deduct?

Generally, all qualifying research expenditures of a current nature may be deducted in full in the year in which they are incurred. However, a current year deduction will not be permitted for accrued amounts that are not paid within 180 days of the end of the taxation year. In addition, subject to the available-for-use rules (see article 7), new equipment purchased to be used solely for qualifying research in Canada may also be written off in the year it is acquired. As a rule, expenditures incurred to acquire or rent a building do not qualify as scientific research expenditures.

TAX TIP

You don't have to claim the full amount of eligible SR&ED expenses in the year in which they were incurred. It may make better business sense to carry forward and deduct the amounts in a subsequent year. However, to deduct an amount for SR&ED, you must be carrying on the business to which the research relates in the year in which you make the claim. For example, in some years you might not want to claim a deduction if it will increase a non-capital loss, since the carry-forward will expire in seven years. By the same token, it might be advantageous to carry forward the deduction to a year in which it can be claimed against a higher marginal tax rate.

Claiming SR&ED

To claim special treatment for scientific research expenditures, you must complete Form T661. This requires you to provide a breakdown of the expenditures made, as well as details of the types of projects undertaken, such as the scientific or technological content, advancements made, and uncertainties pursued. It is vital that project descriptions are complete. Failure to describe the projects properly could result in a rejection of the claim or, at best, it could significantly delay processing.

Outlays will not qualify for the beneficial tax treatment afforded research and development expenditures unless form T661 is filed within 12 months of the due date for filing for the taxation year. In other words, if a corporation with a December 31 year-end incurs SR&ED expenditures, form T661 (for the 2001 taxation year) must be filed by June 30, 2003. That's because the due date for filing the corporate income tax return is June 30, 2002, six months from the December 31, 2001, year-end.

Not all the news from the tax department means more complications for you. A new application form was recently introduced to streamline the paperwork required for small businesses (Form T665), but only certain corporations will be eligible to use this simplified form. Your tax adviser can assess whether you qualify.

Investment tax credit

Both current and capital expenditures on scientific research also qualify for a business investment tax credit (ITC). For example, if you own a small Canadian-controlled private corporation (CCPC) that incurs $100,000 of qualifying scientific expenditures, your company can claim an investment tax credit of $35,000 ($100,000 × 35%). This amount is first deducted from your company's federal taxes payable for the year. If there is any amount remaining, the excess can generate a refund. You can carry unused credits back up to three years or forward up to 10 years.

Currently, this refundable system is available only to individuals and certain CCPCs. SR&ED ITCs earned at the 35% rate are eligible for a 100% refund if the ITC relates to current SR&ED expenditures. In all other cases, the refundable portion is equal to 40% of the unused credits.

ITCs either reduce the tax cost of the related asset or are included in income in the year following the year the credit is claimed.

A CCPC is eligible for the 35% tax credit rate on up to $2 million of qualifying SR&ED expenditures in the year, provided taxable income did not exceed $200,000 and taxable capital did not exceed $10 million in the preceding year. A CCPC whose taxable income for the preceding year was between $200,000 and $400,000 or whose taxable capital was between $10 million and $15 million will also be eligible for the 35% rate. However the $2-million limit on qualifying expenses will be reduced.

When determining eligibility for this rate of credit, the taxable income and taxable capital include those of the corporation and all associated corporations. Corporations and individuals not eligible for the 35% rate can earn credits at the rate of 20%.

Due date for filing

In order to claim an ITC, a completed form giving details of the qualifying cost or expense must be filed within 12 months of the due date of the return for the taxation year in which the ITC arises. This filing deadline is the same as the one for scientific SR&ED expenditures. The details are reported on Schedule 31.

TAX TIP

To qualify for an ITC, you must make sure all current SR&ED expenditures are paid within 180 days of the year-end.

TAX TIP

In the case of equipment that is used only partially for SR&ED, the cost may not be written off as an eligible SR&ED expenditure. However, if the equipment is used primarily (more than 50%) for SR&ED, the cost may be eligible for a reduced ITC. For equipment to qualify for a tax credit, the equipment must be new.

Overhead expenses

Much of the Income Tax Act can be said to be confounding, but one area that has always caused confusion is in the determination of eligible SR&ED overhead expenses. To simplify matters, you have the option of calculating eligible overhead expenses using a simple formula based on wages and salaries, and the amount arrived at in this manner is called the "proxy amount." In general, this amount is calculated as 65% of the portion of salaries or wages of employees directly engaged in SR&ED in Canada.

The proxy amount is added to the expenses eligible for an ITC. However, it does not increase the amount of SR&ED expenditures available for deduction. Again, there are special rules that limit the amount of salary to be used in the calculation. These apply if that salary has been paid to an employee who does not deal at arm's length with the taxpayer, or to an employee who owns or is related to someone who owns 10% or more of the shares of the employer corporation.

TAX TIP

The use of the "proxy amount" is elective and, if you choose to use this method for a particular year, the election must be made at the time form T661 is first filed for that year.

Provincial incentives

A number of investment tax credits and other tax incentives for SR&ED are offered by several of the provinces, and the qualifying activities must be carried out in the province that grants these tax breaks.

TAX TIP

Not incorporated? Here's another reason to consider it. If you are carrying on a business and conduct scientific research that relates to that business, you should consider incorporating. The provincial incentives, as well as the 35% ITC rate, are only available to corporations.

The rules involved in claiming scientific SR&ED expenditures and related investment tax credits are extremely complex. Consult with your tax adviser to ensure you get the maximum benefit from these tax incentives.

36 Shareholder agreements

If your corporation has more than one shareholder, a shareholders' agreement should be drawn up to establish the ongoing rights and responsibilities of the shareholders in the ownership and administration of the company.

In the event of death...

One of the more important aspects of the shareholders' agreement is that it should specify what should happen in the event of the death or disability of one of the shareholders. Not only will this provide for a smooth transition of the business, but such agreements generally establish a purchaser for the shares of the deceased, a formula for determining the purchase price, and a method for funding the purchase. By arranging proper tax planning, the buyout can be orchestrated to minimize a drain on cash flow for the company and for survivors. A sound arrangement can also minimize or defer the tax liability of the estate.

The most efficient means of funding a buy-sell agreement or share repurchase on the death of a shareholder is generally through life insurance. However, the use of corporate-owned life insurance to fund a share repurchase may no longer be an effective tax strategy. It is highly recommended that you speak with your tax adviser to develop a plan that is appropriate to your situation.

TAX TIP

In 1995, the government enacted changes that can significantly alter the tax implications where life insurance proceeds are used to fund a share repurchase. One of the things that should be at the top of your agenda is to undertake a review of your shareholders' agreement. That way, you can ensure your objectives are met in the most tax-effective manner.

37 Reporting system for contractors

If you are in the construction business and make payments to subcontractors, you have to report certain payments to the CCRA.

Who must report?

All businesses whose principal activity is construction—whether carried out by an individual, partnership, or corporation—are required to report. For this purpose, construction is defined as erecting, installing, altering, modifying, repairing, improving, demolishing, dismantling, or removing any structure or part thereof.

What payments must be reported?

You must report payments to subcontractors if the amount paid for construction services is $500 or more. Payments for goods are not included in determining whether a payment satisfies this test, and the payments can be reported on either a calendar-year or fiscal-year basis. For example, your business's year-end is June 30, 2001. Your reporting return for 2001 can either report all payments made from July 1, 2000, to June 30, 2001, or it can report all payments made from January 1, 2001, to December 31, 2001.

What information must be reported?

If you are involved in the construction business and pay a subcontractor for services rendered, you must report the name of the subcontractor, the business address, the subcontractor's business number (BN) or social insurance number (if no BN is available), and the amount paid for the reporting period.

The information can be reported on either a Contract Payment Reporting Information return (form T5018) or, alternatively, the information can be reported on a line-by-line basis in a column format with the appropriate summary information.

In general, the due date for filing the required information is six months from the end of the reporting period.

Although you are not required to provide any information slips to the subcontractors, it is reasonable to assume that they will want to know what information is being reported to the CCRA.

TAX TIP

If you are in the construction business and pay subcontractors for work performed, be sure to obtain all the necessary information to complete the information return and file it on a timely basis.

38 Transfer pricing

A transfer price is a price charged between related parties involved in international transactions—for example, where a Canadian resident buys goods and services from or sells products to a related non-resident corporation. The government's concern centres on ensuring that the price charged is equal to the amount that would be agreed upon by parties dealing at arm's length. If it is not, taxable profits may be shifted from one jurisdiction to another.

Recent legislation on transfer pricing mirrors laws that have been put in place in other industrialized countries such as the United States, the United Kingdom, and Australia. It requires Canadian taxpayers to adopt the arm's-length principle in setting transfer prices for transactions with related non-resident persons and to document the basis of the transfer pricing.

The arm's-length principle has always been required in transactions with related persons, but the new, more specific requirement applies for tax years commencing after 1997. Documentation standards are applicable for tax years commencing after 1998 and stipulate that the documentation for a particular tax year be completed by the due date for filing that year's tax return. Failure to complete the documentation can result in a penalty of 10% of the transfer pricing adjustment. And the penalty can apply even though no additional tax arises as a result of the transfer pricing adjustment.

TAX TIP

If you have transactions with related non-resident persons, have your tax adviser review your transfer pricing polices, as well as related documentation, to determine whether they comply with the transfer pricing legislation.

39 Thin capitalization rules

The thin capitalization rules are designed to prevent non-residents of Canada who own shares in Canadian resident corporations from withdrawing profits in the form of interest payments that are subject to a low rate of withholding tax. These rules limit the amount of interest a Canadian corporation can deduct when the amount of outstanding debts payable to specified non-resident shareholders exceeds a certain amount.

In general, a "specified shareholder" is a shareholder who, either alone or together with persons with whom he is not dealing at arm's length, owns 25% or more of the issued shares of any class of the corporation.

Prior to 2001, if the debt to such persons exceeded three times the "equity" of the Canadian resident corporation, a prorated portion of the interest paid or payable in the year to the non-residents was not allowed as a deduction in computing the income of the Canadian resident corporation.

For tax years commencing after 2000, significant changes have been made to these rules. The most significant of these is that the debt-to-equity ratio has been reduced from 3:1 to 2:1. Important changes also apply to the computation of the equity component of the formula. Most importantly, it will no longer be possible for corporations to correct an equity deficiency by having specified non-residents subscribe for additional share capital immediately prior to year-end.

TAX TIP

If your corporation pays interest to specified non-residents, contact your tax adviser to determine if it is subject to these rules and whether planning strategies could reduce or eliminate their impact.

40 The goods on the GST/HST

In 1991, the 7% GST replaced the old federal sales tax as a consumption tax on most goods and services provided in Canada. However, unlike provincial retail sales taxes that are imposed only at the time of a sale to a consumer, the GST is a multi-level tax collected every time a taxable good or service is provided. Businesses that charge GST on their revenues can recover GST paid on related expenses by claiming an "input tax credit" so they bear no net tax.

In 1997, Newfoundland and Labrador, New Brunswick, and Nova Scotia replaced their respective provincial sales taxes and harmonized them with the federal GST to create the harmonized sales tax (HST). The HST operates in the same manner and is generally applicable to the same base of goods and services as the GST. However, it is applied at a rate of 15%.

Supplies of goods or services are taxed in three ways. Most goods and services are rated as taxable supplies and attract tax at 7% outside the HST-participating provinces and 15% in the provinces using the HST. While you don't have to keep track of how much tax is collected at 7% or 15%, creating a supporting audit trail is highly recommended. All tax collected must be remitted. Any GST/HST–registered business that makes only taxable supplies recovers all the GST/HST it pays as an input tax credit. Tax is not collected on zero-rated supplies, but full input tax credits are claimed for the GST/HST paid on related inputs. Zero-rated supplies include most basic foods, agricultural products, prescription drugs, medical devices, and most goods and services that are exported.

Exempt supplies are not subject to GST/HST, but a business making them is not entitled to claim an input tax credit for the GST/HST on related costs. In effect, a business making exempt supplies bears the cost of the GST/HST and must factor it into the price of the goods and services sold. Long-term residential rents, health care, and financial services are the most common types of exempt supplies.

41 GST/HST registration, collection, and remittance

Unless a business has $30,000 or more in annual taxable sales, it is not required to register and collect tax, but take into account the fact that worldwide revenues of associated entities are included in measuring annual taxable sales. Businesses not required to register are called "small suppliers." Such businesses can elect to register and collect tax, as this enables them to claim input tax credits for any GST/HST they pay on purchases (see article 42). Generally, this is advisable if the recipient of the supply is also registered for the tax.

Separate thresholds are used to determine whether charities and public sector bodies are required to register.

New businesses

Starting a new business venture? Then it is usually a good idea to register for GST/HST as soon as possible. Early registration ensures that GST/HST paid on costs incurred is recoverable, since any tax paid prior to registration can generally be recovered only on the purchase of inventory, capital property, and prepaid services still on hand at the time of registration. In certain situations, late registration can sometimes result in not being able to recover GST/HST paid prior to registration. So register early!

When to report

Every business has a reporting period based on its revenue. Most businesses are required to report quarterly. However, large businesses (over $6 million in annual taxable supplies) must report monthly, while small businesses (under $500,000 in annual taxable supplies) may elect to report on an annual basis. New GST/HST registrants with annual taxable supplies of under $500,000 are automatically assigned an annual reporting period unless they choose to file more frequently.

TAX TIP

You can elect to report more frequently than required. This is advisable if you are generally in a net refund position, as businesses that sell a large percentage of zero-rated goods often are.

Certain businesses that have either a nil balance or a refund of $10,000 or less can now use TELEFILE to file their GST/HST returns.

42 Input tax credits

If you have paid GST/HST on goods and services used in making taxable and zero-rated supplies, you can claim input tax credits. To ensure your claim will be allowed, you must have supporting documentation in your records in case your claim is ever challenged. You should go over the detailed rules that govern the content of this supporting documentation thoroughly and make sure you comply with each stipulation. Audit problems often arise through deficient documentation, even if the deficiency is minor.

If input tax credits claimed in a reporting period exceed the tax owing, the excess is refunded to the business.

Shorter time frame for some claims

Registrants that are listed financial institutions and certain registrants whose taxable supplies for the preceding two years (including the supplies of associated businesses) exceed $6 million have only two years to claim input tax credits. The CCRA, on the other hand, still has four years to audit a GST/HST return. Therefore, it is essential that such large businesses ensure their systems accurately and completely capture and claim all

GST/HST paid. Generally, businesses in which 90% of their supplies are taxable in either of the two immediately preceding fiscal years are excluded from the two-year restriction, as are charities. These and all other registrants maintain the ability to claim input tax credits for four years.

Allocation of tax between taxable and exempt supplies

Businesses that make both taxable and exempt supplies must allocate the tax paid on purchases between the two types of supplies. Any reasonable method of allocation is acceptable, and it is not necessary to use the same method from year to year, though the same method must be used consistently during the course of the year. The allocation of input tax credits allows you some scope for planning.

EXAMPLE

A GST registrant involved in both taxable and exempt activities incurs GST of $3,200 in respect to occupancy costs. If 70% of the total floor space is used in commercial activities, based upon the square footage, the registrant may choose to use this allocation method and claim $2,240 (70% × $3,200) as an input tax credit. Alternatively, the registrant may choose to base the allocation on the number of employees working in each particular activity.

TAX TIP

A business that must allocate the tax paid on purchases of both taxable and exempt supplies to claim input tax credits should review its allocation method each year. Due to inherent changes in business activity, it may be advantageous to change the allocation method, since this may result in a higher recoverable percentage.

43 GST/HST and automobiles

The complexity of the automobile rules is taken a step further by the GST/HST factor.

Passenger vehicles that cost more than a prescribed amount (currently $30,000, net of GST and PST or HST) are included in a separate depreciable class identified as class 10.1. For passenger vehicles acquired after 2000, the input tax credit is limited to the tax on $30,000, excluding PST and GST or HST. That means the maximum input tax credit for passenger vehicles subject to the 7% GST is $2,100. In Nova Scotia, New Brunswick, and Newfoundland and Labrador, where a harmonized tax has been established, the maximum tax credit available is $4,500.

Special rules apply to GST/HST–registered individuals and partnerships where the vehicle is not used more than 90% in a commercial activity. Generally, GST/HST is recovered based on annual deductible capital cost allowance claims. Upon the subsequent sale of the vehicle, it may be possible to recapture a portion of the unclaimed GST.

EXAMPLE

GST and your auto

You are self-employed and registered for the GST. You purchase an automobile for $28,000, including GST. You use the vehicle 60% in commercial activities and 40% for personal use, based upon the kilometres driven in the year. The maximum capital cost allowance you can claim in the year of purchase is $2,520 ($\frac{1}{2} \times 30\% \times \$28,000 \times 60\%$).

Because you use the automobile less than 90% in commercial activities, for GST purposes you may claim an input tax credit of $165 ($\frac{7}{107} \times \$2,520$), assuming the maximum capital cost allowance is claimed. If you live in a province that is subject to the HST, the recoverable factor is $\frac{15}{115}$.

And if all that isn't enough, the GST/HST must also be considered if a vehicle is sold or traded in—and the rules differ depending on the status of the vendor. Is the vendor registered for the GST/HST? Is the vendor a corporation, individual, or partnership? Your tax adviser can help you avoid any pitfalls in this regard.

GST/HST also has to be considered if you provide your employees with a vehicle for their personal use or pay for any of the vehicle's operating expenses (see article 31). If your company is a GST/HST registrant, the resulting taxable benefit is deemed to be a taxable supply and GST/HST must be remitted on the benefit amount. Your company must remit the tax on its GST/HST return that covers the last day of February each year—in other words, for the period that includes the due date for filing T4 slips for the relevant year. The GST/HST with respect to vehicles provided to shareholders who are not employees must be reported on the GST/HST return that includes the last day of the taxation year.

How much do you owe?

The GST/HST to be remitted is calculated by formula and, surprisingly, not directly tied to the actual amount paid. The formula varies with the nature of the benefit and whether the employee or shareholder being taxed on the benefit works or lives in a participating province. The remittance is calculated as follows:

	Standby charge	Operating cost benefit
Outside participating provinces	$6/106$	5%
Participating provinces, 1998 and later	$14/114$	11%

TAX TIP

If personal use of the automobile is high and the employee or shareholder incurs most but not all of the operating costs, the taxable operating cost benefit and related GST/HST remittance may be higher than the portion of actual operating costs paid by the employer. It's a good idea to review employment arrangements from time to time to determine whether it's time to make changes.

EXAMPLE

An automobile is made available to an employee in a non-participating province, and that individual drives 14,000 personal kilometres and only 6,000 business kilometres in the year. The employer pays only $500 of the operating costs and the employee pays the remainder. An operating cost benefit of $2,240 (16¢ per personal kilometre) must be reported and the employer must remit $112 of GST on the benefit ($2,240 × 5%).

Finally, certain employees and partners may be able to claim a GST/HST rebate for particular expenses that are deductible in computing income for tax purposes. The rules in this area are complex as well. For example, if you receive a tax-free travel allowance you include in income and claim offsetting expenses, you cannot claim the rebate. A GST/HST–registered employer, however, is entitled to claim a notional input tax credit for the amount paid. The rules are just the reverse if you receive a travel allowance that has to be included in income—for example, a flat allowance of $400 a month. You may be able to claim the rebate, but the employer cannot claim an input tax credit. This rebate is calculated as $7/107$ of eligible expenses in those provinces subject to the GST and generally as $15/115$ of eligible expenses in those provinces subject to the HST. Although you can file the rebate claim with your personal tax return, you have up to four years to make a claim. To claim the rebate, the employer must be registered for GST/HST and cannot be a listed financial institution such as a bank, credit union, insurance company, or an investment or insurance brokerage.

44 GST/HST and real property sales

As a general rule, real property sales are taxable even when the vendor is a small supplier. In such cases, the vendor must collect and remit the tax (unless the purchaser is a GST/HST registrant—see discussion below). Major exemptions are the sale of used residential property and the sale of real property by an individual who is not engaged in a business. However, if the property has been subdivided into more than two parts, even an individual must charge the tax when the property is sold unless the property is specifically exempt, such as used residential property.

Sales of real property to a registrant

A vendor is generally not required to collect the tax where real property is sold to a GST/HST registrant. A business selling real property should ensure that the purchaser is a GST/HST registrant before concluding not to collect tax on the sale. The GST/HST is still payable, but the purchaser is obligated to remit the tax. If the property is used in making taxable supplies, the offsetting input tax credit can usually be claimed on the same reporting return that reports the liability.

TAX TIP

When a non-registrant sells real property, and the deal is subject to tax, the vendor can claim back any GST/HST previously paid on the acquisition or improvement of the property that has not already been recovered. The eligible amount is claimed back by filing a rebate form. If the vendor collects tax on the sale, the result is that the vendor sends the CCRA the net amount of the tax collected less the rebate amount. If the vendor does not collect tax on the sale (because the purchaser is registered), the rebate will be paid directly by the CCRA. The rebate application must be filed within two years of the date of sale.

45 GST/HST and buying and selling a business

A purchaser and vendor may be able to file a special election to avoid paying GST/HST when business assets are sold. This election is usually available if the purchaser is acquiring ownership or use of all the property needed to carry on that business or a part of that business. The big difficulty arises as you try to determine if the business assets being sold qualify for this election. Before signing the papers, you should consult with your tax adviser about the advisability of seeking a ruling from CCRA.

46 GST/HST audits

Although this tax has been making the lives of many Canadians a little more complicated since its inception in 1991, most of its technical provisions have yet to be tested in the courts. Furthermore, the CCRA's administrative policies continue to evolve as it gains more experience with the tax.

As with income tax audits, prevention is always better than a cure. A comprehensive review of systems and compliance can often resolve problems before the auditor identifies them. Many audit adjustments generate only interest and penalty payments—failure to collect tax on a sale may often be offset by an input tax credit to the recipient unless the expense relates to the recipient's exempt supplies. In most cases, the CCRA's policy is to allow the interest and penalties to be reduced to a penalty equal to 4% of the net amount of the tax owing on these transactions. A registrant does not have to apply for such relief. The tax department's published policy is to provide the relief on assessment. In some cases, where the assessment or reassessment results from a voluntary disclosure, the 4% penalty may also be waived.

47 Residential rental property rebate

In certain situations, a GST/HST rebate can now be claimed by landlords and builders of residential property intended for rental. This rebate applies to construction, substantial renovation, or conversions begun after February 27, 2000, and mirrors the relief currently available under the new housing rebate program—i.e., a full rebate of 2.5% of the GST/HST payable on units valued up to $350,000, a reduced rebate between $350,000 and $450,000, and no rebate on units valued at $450,000 or more. Generally, rebates may be claimed up to two years from the end of the month in which the tax becomes payable.

Individuals

ndividuals face a tough challenge in learning the many tax implications affecting them and then developing ways to deal with them. However, many pitfalls can be readily avoided with proper tax planning. A thorough assessment of your circumstances will no doubt uncover a number of ways to reduce your tax liability.

In this section, we address about 60 of the most common areas that can affect your tax position, both positively and negatively, and give details on the various credits you can claim—many of which are often not used because many Canadians aren't aware that these tax relief measures are available to them.

We've also included a dozen or so items describing the rules and the inherent versatility of one of Canada's best tax reduction tools—the registered retirement savings plan—as well as up-to-date information on the changes to the rules and the improved attractiveness of registered education saving plans.

Other areas covered include the tax implications of owning more than one piece of real estate, how you can reduce your tax load by splitting income with family members, what's involved in becoming a Canadian resident, and by the same token what happens when you give up your Canadian residency. Last but certainly not least are details on one of the most overlooked but vitally important areas for you to consider—estate planning.

And, of course, we've been sure to include numerous tips to help you make smart choices as you draw up a tax strategy for your particular circumstances.

48 Filing a tax return

You are required to file an income tax return for a taxation year if you:

- have tax payable for that year

- sold or disposed of capital property in the year
- have to repay Old Age Security or employment insurance benefits
- want to apply for the goods and services tax or harmonized sales tax credit
- want to apply for the Old Age Security supplement
- have self-employed earnings of $3,500 or more in the year and must make CPP contributions, even if your income is otherwise below taxable levels
- receive a demand from the CCRA to file a return

In addition, you and your spouse or common-law partner must file a return if you want to receive payments under the Canada child tax benefit system.

TAX TIP

Anyone, including minors, with "earned income" for RRSP purposes should consider filing an income tax return. Your contribution room, which may be used in subsequent years, will only accumulate if a tax return is filed (see article **55**).

49 Your return is due...

Most individuals are required to mail their income tax returns on or before April 30 of the following calendar year. In other words, your 2001 return will be due by April 30, 2002. This date is particularly important if you owe the government a tax payment. Penalties on outstanding amounts begin to accumulate after that deadline. If the government owes you a refund, it doesn't make any sense to wait until that date—much less past that date. File as soon as you have all your documentation. After all, the refund is your money, and it's not doing you a lot of good sitting in the treasury.

There is an exception to the above rule. If you or your spouse or common-law partner carry on a business (other than as a member of a limited partnership) during the year, you have until June 15 of the following year to file your return.

EXAMPLE
Due dates

If you and your spouse were both employed full-time, and your spouse also had a part-time consulting business in 2001, you both have until June 15, 2002, to file your returns. However, any tax owing by you and your spouse must be paid by April 30, 2002.

TAX TIP

Anticipating a refund? Then you should still file your return as early as possible. Interest on refunds will only be paid from June 15 or 45 days after you file your return, whichever is the latest date.

50 GST/HST credit

The GST/HST credit is intended to offset GST/HST paid by lower-income individuals and families during the year and is paid in quarterly instalments following the due date for filing a return. Since a 2001 return is generally due by April 30, 2002, the quarterly payments will be scheduled for July and October 2002 and January and April 2003.

Subject to income restrictions, you are eligible to claim the credit. However, at the end of the year, you must be a resident of Canada and either 19 years of age or over, married, or a parent. No credit can be claimed for a person who died during the year.

What's it worth?

For 2001, the basic GST/HST credit for an individual is $207. For families, the credit is $207 for you and $207 for your spouse or common-law partner (or other parent of your child). An eligible child will be credited with $109. If you are married and living with your spouse or common-law partner (or other parent of your child), only one of you may claim the credit for the family unit. It does not matter which of you claims.

However, the total credit you may claim is reduced by 5% of your combined adjusted net incomes in excess of a specified threshold amount, which is $26,941 for 2001. Therefore, a married couple with two eligible children will qualify for the full credit of $632 if their combined family income is $26,941 or less. Their entitlement will decrease to zero once family income exceeds $39,581.

To apply for the GST credit, you must file an income tax return—even if you have no income to report. Individuals 19 years of age or older at the end of 2001 must apply for their own credits by filing a tax return.

51 Why buy an RRSP?

There are three compelling reasons for contributing to a registered retirement savings plan, or RRSP. First, your contribution is tax deductible—and the higher your marginal tax rate, the greater your tax savings. Second, the income generated by the plan is only taxed on withdrawal from the plan (usually when you are retired and possibly in a lower tax bracket). That means you can build up quite significant earnings inside your plan on a pre-tax basis. Finally, all or a portion of your annual eligible contribution can be contributed to a plan set up for your spouse or common-law partner.

Spousal plans

Setting up a spousal RRSP is a good idea if you expect your spouse or common-law partner to be in a lower tax bracket than you on retirement. When your spouse or common-law partner withdraws funds from the spousal RRSP, they are taxed in his or her hands at a lower rate (this arrangement is subject to special rules to prevent abuse), which reduces your family's total tax bill. This strategy also means that benefits such as the pension credit can be made available to both of you, and you may reduce your exposure to the old age security clawback (see article **66**).

The majority of Canadians do not focus on retirement planning early in their careers. Yet contributing to an RRSP as early as possible, even if not to the maximum allowable amount, is a very powerful retirement planning strategy. Once you invest in an RRSP, you can earn income that compounds on a pre-tax basis. Depending on the type of investment products in your RRSP, this additional growth can often be far more substantial than the initial savings realized through the tax deduction.

If you don't have an RRSP, don't worry, you're not alone. Despite the many benefits of an RRSP, many Canadians don't have one. However, you *should* fret about missing out on reducing your taxes and creating a substantial retirement nest egg that compounds tax-free. RRSPs are not at all hard to establish. Talk to a financial planner or your bank's financial services staff, who can set up an RRSP with a minimum of fuss or confusion. As for the type of RRSP to select, you should give consideration to a self-directed plan—you don't really have to manage it, but it gives you much more flexibility in your financial and tax-planning strategies (see article **56**).

52 How much can you contribute?

Your maximum annual RRSP contribution is based on earned income in the previous year. Earned income includes salaries, business income, disability pensions (issued under the Canada and Quebec pension plans), taxable alimony/maintenance, and rental income. Remember, too, your earned income is reduced by business losses, rental losses, and deductible alimony/maintenance paid. Retiring allowances, investment income, capital gains, and pension income are not classified as earned income.

Estimating your contribution limit

If you are not a member of a registered pension plan (RPP) or a deferred profit sharing plan (DPSP), you will be able to contribute 18% of your year 2000 earned income to an RRSP in 2001—up to a maximum of $13,500. That contribution must be made by March 1, 2002.

If you were not able to make the maximum contribution to your plan in any or all the years from 1991 to 2000, you can also make up the difference in 2001 (see article **55**). Your 2001 earned income will determine your 2002 contribution limit.

Making the maximum RRSP contribution in 2001 will require earned income of at least $75,000 for 2000. To find out how much you can contribute, check the Notice of Assessment that the CCRA sent you after your 2000 return was processed. It will tell you how much you can contribute. This amount should take into account any under-contributions since 1991.

RPP, DPSP members

If you are a member of an RPP or DPSP, your RRSP contribution limit will be reduced by an amount called the pension adjustment (PA). This adjustment represents the present value of the pension benefits you earned for the previous year in your RPP or DPSP. PA reporting is required as part of the T4 reporting process in February of each year.

Another thing to consider is an adjustment made where benefits are enhanced for post-1989 service. This particular adjustment—the past service pension adjustment (PSPA)—reduces your RRSP contribution limit for any given year. In general, your maximum deduction for any one year will be calculated as follows: RRSP contribution room carried forward (see article **55**), plus 18% of your prior year's earned income (to a stated maximum), plus any pension adjustment reversal (PAR—see below), less your PA for the prior year, less any PSPA for the current year.

EXAMPLE

Adjustments and your RRSP

If your earned income for 2000 was $40,000, and a PA of $2,200 was reported on your 2000 T4, you will be able to contribute $5,000 to an RRSP in 2001: 18% of $40,000 = $7,200 less the $2,200 PA. However, if a $3,000 PSPA was also reported on slip T215, you would only be able to contribute $2,000 to your RRSP in 2001: 18% of $40,000 = $7,200 less the $2,200 PA and less the $3,000 PSPA.

Pension adjustment reversals

If members of an RPP or DPSP leave before retirement, the pension entitlement they receive is often less than the RRSP contribution room they gave up in favour of the pension plan. Recognizing this inequity, the government introduced a pension adjustment reversal (PAR) that is intended to restore lost RRSP contribution room to individuals who leave an RPP or DPSP before retirement.

Generally, the PAR increases the RRSP contribution limit by the amount by which the PAs exceed the termination benefit—thereby restoring the RRSP room that would otherwise be lost. The PAR applies for terminations in 1997 and subsequent years, and RPP or DPSP administrators are required to report the PAR to the CCRA. The PAR is added to the RRSP deduction room for the year of termination.

EXAMPLE
Applying the PAR

Suppose you were laid off by your employer in 2000 and, based on your earned income for that year, your 2001 RRSP contribution room was $13,500. If your former employer reports a PAR of $5,000 with respect to your participation in its pension plan, your 2001 RRSP deduction room will be increased to $18,500.

Age limits

Subject to age restrictions, you may contribute any amount up to your maximum to your RRSP, an RRSP set up for your spouse or common-law partner, or a combination of both. A contribution cannot be made to an RRSP if the beneficiary of the RRSP is 70 years of age or older at the end of the year. However, if you have earned income and your spouse or common-law partner will be under 70 at the end of the year, you can still make a contribution to his or her plan even if you are 70 or older.

Converting your RRSP

Normally, you have until March 1, 2002, to make your 2001 contribution. However, if the beneficiary of the plan turned 69 in 2001, the contribution must be made by December 31, 2001. That's because RRSPs must be converted into a registered retirement income fund (RRIF) or life or term annuity by December 31 of the year in which the beneficiary turns 69.

A huge word of warning—if you turned 69 in 2001, and your RRSP is not converted into one of these plans by December 31, 2001, the full amount of the RRSP will be brought into your income, and you could incur a substantial tax bill on the additional income. Not only that, your entitlement to Old Age Security benefits may be drastically reduced.

For a taxpayer who dies in 2001, the executor or legal representative can make a spousal RRSP contribution on behalf of the deceased until March 1, 2002.

If you turned 69 in 2001, you may be able to make an extra contribution for 2002 to your RRSP before collapsing the plan at the end of 2001. Just before you wind it up in 2001, make a contribution equal to your 2002 contribution room. The amount of your 2002 contribution room is based on your 2001 earned income. Payments can then be claimed as a deduction in 2002. This tax-planning tip requires that you have contribution room available for 2002 (i.e., based on your 2001 earned income), and you should discuss it with your tax adviser before proceeding. It is important to note that the contribution may trigger a 1% per month penalty from the date of the contribution to December 31, 2001 (see article **54**). Therefore, it would be wise to make this extra contribution in December 2001.

Before proceeding with this option, you and your tax adviser should review your financial situation carefully in light of your contribution room, the amount of the contribution, the penalty tax, etc. You still have the opportunity in the future to contribute to a spousal RRSP if you have earned income and your spouse or common-law partner is under 70 years of age.

53 RRSP contribution limits

The RRSP contribution limit is currently $13,500 and will remain at this level until 2003. After that time, it will be increased to $14,500 in 2004 and $15,500 in 2005. For money purchase RPPs, the maximum limits are also frozen at $13,500 until 2002. After that, the limit will rise to $14,500 in 2003 and $15,500 in 2004. Contributions to defined benefit RPPs are not restricted by dollar amounts but the entitlement under such plans is limited to defined levels that approximate the limits for money purchase RPPs.

After 2004 (2005 for RRSPs), the maximum limits are to be adjusted for the annual increase in the average industrial wage.

To make the most effective use of your RRSP, there are several things you can and should do. It's a good idea to contribute to your RRSP early rather than at the end of the contribution year—that way you can take advantage of income sheltering and compounding a full year earlier. If you make regular contributions to an RRSP, consider applying to have your income tax withholdings reduced on your paycheque—this will improve your monthly cash flow. Even though your RRSP administration fee is no longer tax deductible, you should consider paying it directly rather than inside your RRSP—this helps maintain capital in your plan, allowing it to grow on a tax-deferred basis. You do not need to deduct your contribution in the year it is made. If you are expecting to be in a higher tax bracket in the future, consider delaying your deduction until that time—you will receive a larger tax savings if the deduction is taken when you are in a higher tax bracket. And last but not least, consider filing tax returns for children or other low-income earners to create contribution room that may be used in the future.

54 RRSP overcontributions

Starting with the 1991 tax year, individuals 18 years of age or over were allowed to overcontribute a cumulative lifetime total of $8,000 to their RRSP without incurring a penalty tax. However, as of January 1, 1996, this allowable limit was reduced to $2,000, with an additional allowance provided to an individual who had an overcontribution on February 26, 1995.

An overcontribution is not deductible from income in the current year, but the advantage lies in the fact that you can inject extra cash into your RRSP, where it can compound on a pre-tax basis for as long as it remains in the plan. Overcontributions may be deducted in a subsequent year when an actual contribution is less than the maximum allowed. As of January 1, 1996, the penalty tax of 1% per month applies to the amount of any overcontribution in excess of $2,000, subject to the exception for the additional allowance.

Know your limit

An additional allowance is provided for individuals who had an overcontribution on February 26, 1995. If an overcontribution in excess of $2,000 existed on that date, the monthly penalty tax will not be imposed, provided the overcontribution did not exceed $8,000 and it is used against available RRSP contribution room for 1996 and subsequent years until the overcontribution is reduced to $2,000.

TAX TIP

Before overcontributing to an RRSP, you are usually better off to pay down debt on which interest is not deductible, such as a large outstanding personal credit card balance or a personal home mortgage. Check with your tax or financial adviser to determine your best course of action. If you do decide to overcontribute, work with your adviser to ensure you stay within the allowable limit. One of the reasons the government permits an overcontribution is to provide you with a cushion against possible errors and unforeseen events.

TAX TIP

Consider using your $2,000 overcontribution when you quit working. The earned income you have in your final year of employment will entitle you to an RRSP deduction in the following year.

55 RRSP carry-forward rules

For many individuals, it is not always possible to make a full RRSP contribution in any given year. To remedy this situation, you are allowed to carry forward the unused portion of your contribution room to subsequent years. If you were eligible to contribute $10,000 to an RRSP each year from 1991 to 2000 but contributed only $7,000 each year, you will be able to contribute an additional $30,000 over and above your annual maximum contribution limit.

If you expect a change in your income in the near future—a change that might see you bumped up into a higher tax bracket—it might make sense to consider delaying your RRSP contributions until that time. However, you must also consider the loss of tax-sheltered investment growth by building up your RRSP later rather than earlier.

TAX TIP

In order to accumulate RRSP contribution room, you must file an income tax return. If you have earned income for RRSP purposes but are not required to file an income tax return, you should consider filing one anyway. While an RRSP may not be a significant consideration at this point, there will probably be a time when you have sufficient cash to make a contribution and benefit from the deduction.

TAX TIP

Will you have low taxable income in 2001, unused contribution room, and enough excess cash to make an RRSP contribution? Then consider making the contribution for 2001 but not claiming the deduction on that year's return. As long as the amount is not claimed as a deduction, your unused contribution room will remain intact. You can still claim the deduction in a future year, preferably when your taxable income is higher. In the meantime, the investments in the RRSP will compound tax-free.

56 Self-directed RRSPs

Self-directed RRSPs are subject to special rules. Despite the annual administration fee—which unfortunately is not tax deductible—a self-directed RRSP will give you more flexibility and may provide you with the opportunity to realize better returns. However, you should have a little time to give it the attention it needs.

In a self-directed plan, you make your own investment choices. These decisions can be based on information given to you by your tax or financial adviser. In fact, many Canadians allow their financial planners to look after their self-directed plans. However, as the owner of the plan, you always have the final say in how it is managed and the types of investments purchased.

Should your plan acquire an investment that does not meet the qualifications, the value of that investment is included as income on your return. Additional taxes may apply on foreign property acquired by the plan. You are also restricted in the amount of foreign investments you can hold in your RRSP. Prior to 2000, the foreign investments that could be held in an RRSP (and other registered plans) were limited to 20%. This limit increased to 25% for 2000 and is 30% for 2001 and subsequent years.

Transferring investments

You may transfer other investments you own into your self-directed RRSP as part of your deductible contribution, or you may sell them to your plan. Should their fair market value at the time of the transfer or sale exceed your cost, the difference must be reported as a capital gain. However, if your cost exceeds the fair market value, you cannot deduct the capital loss. For this reason, it is not a good idea to sell or transfer losing investments to your RRSP. It is also possible to hold the mortgage on your home in your RRSP—it takes a little bit of effort to set up, and there are costs involved, but this arrangement can offer some advantages.

EXAMPLE

Investment transfers

In your quest for financial independence, you acquired 100 shares of ABC Co. in 1998 for $10 per share. Now, a few years later, in December 2001, you are considering a contribution to your RRSP and reviewing your available options. If the shares of ABC are trading at $15 per share and you transfer all of the shares to your RRSP, your RRSP contribution will be $1,500 and you will report a capital gain of $500—in other words, $1,500 less the original $1,000 cost of the investment.

If those shares are trading at $8 per share, your RRSP contribution will be $800 but you will not be able to claim a capital loss of $200 ($800 − $1,000) on the transfer. As an alternative, you could sell your shares and contribute the cash proceeds to your RRSP. That being the case, your RRSP contribution will still be $800, but you may be able to claim the $200 capital loss.

TAX TIP

If you have a self-directed RRSP, transferring some of your non-registered investments to it may be a way to get your annual RRSP deduction without actually laying out any cash. However, there are some drawbacks to holding shares in an RRSP. Since shares generate capital gains and dividend income, which is tax-preferred, it might make more sense to keep these investments outside of your RRSP and fill up your contribution room with investments that generate interest—savings bonds, guaranteed investment certificates (GICs), etc.—which are usually taxed at a less advantaged rate.

In recent years, the types of investments that can be held by your self-directed RRSP have grown. In certain situations, your RRSP can invest in a private Canadian company if it carries on its business primarily in Canada. On the other hand, certain types of business activities do not qualify. The rules are extremely complicated, and you should be aware of how they may affect your potential investment before your RRSP acquires it. Talk to a knowledgeable adviser first.

When considering long-term investments such as five-year GICs within your RRSP, keep in mind that you may have a problem if you need to withdraw the funds before the investment matures.

57 Retiring allowances and RRSPs

Individuals who will receive or have received an amount from their former employers upon dismissal or retirement in 2001 may be eligible to contribute an extra amount to their RRSP or RPP. These retiring allowances are a key item in personal tax planning. They are attractive because they are also deductible for the payer. In addition, amounts transferred to your RRSP or RPP are not taxable until they are withdrawn from the plan.

What amounts are involved?

The maximum amount that can be transferred to your RRSP or RPP is $2,000 times the number of years you worked for your employer before 1996. Also add in $1,500 times the number of years you were employed prior to 1989 in which your employer did not make vested contributions to a registered plan on your behalf. Note that the contribution, which is in addition to your regular contribution limit, must be made to your own retirement plan, and not a spousal plan.

TAX TIP

If the portion of your retiring allowance that is eligible to be transferred to your RRSP is paid directly to your RRSP, you must complete form TD2—a tax deduction waiver in respect of funds to be transferred. This way, your employer will not be obligated to withhold income tax.

58 RRSPs and Loans

Interest on loans taken out to invest in an RRSP is not deductible. Therefore, your investments should be structured to take maximum advantage of the interest deductibility rules.

> **TAX TIP**
>
> Consider cashing in an existing investment to contribute to your RRSP and then borrowing funds to acquire another investment. This way, you receive a deduction for your RRSP contribution, and the interest on the loan for investment purposes is also tax deductible.

59 Transfer of pension income

Are you entitled to a lump-sum payment out of a registered pension plan (RPP) or a deferred profit sharing plan (DPSP)? If you wish, that amount can be contributed to another RPP, DPSP, or RRSP. However, the lump-sum payment must be made directly from one plan to another, and then only if certain conditions are met.

If you want to transfer a lump-sum payment or withdrawal from a foreign plan to your RRSP, you should get professional tax advice. For example, the tax implications of transferring amounts from a U.S. individual retirement account (IRA) to a Canadian RRSP are complex. Have your adviser explore all the options and potential tax obligations of such transfers.

60 Using an RRSP to buy a home

The home buyer's plan allows you to withdraw up to $20,000 from your RRSP as a loan without paying tax upon filing form T1036 to report the withdrawal. Only first-time home buyers are eligible to participate under this plan, unless the special rules for persons with disabilities apply, as discussed below. You are considered to be a first-time buyer if, during the four calendar years prior to the year of withdrawal, and up to 30 days before the withdrawal, neither you nor your spouse or common-law partner owned a home in which either of you resided. Loan repayments must take place over a period of 15 years, or less if desired. If the required repayment is not made, an amount will have to be included as income in the year of the shortfall.

> **TAX TIP**
>
> If you contribute an amount to your RRSP, you cannot make a withdrawal under the home buyer's plan within 90 days of that contribution or your ability to claim a deduction for the contribution may be restricted. As a

general rule, you should make your RRSP contribution more than 90 days before the withdrawal. After a wait of 90 days or more, your deduction may generate a refund, which can then also be applied toward your down payment.

In a related move, if you have money on hand for a down payment and you have accumulated some RRSP contribution room, open up an RRSP. Then you can deposit the money into the plan, wait 90 days, be eligible to participate in the home buyer's program, and at the same time use whatever refund is issued to bolster your original down payment amount. Be sure to run this by your tax adviser to ensure that it is a sound strategy for your particular financial circumstances.

If you previously participated in the home buyer's plan, there are certain specified circumstances in which you are able to participate a second time. The provision is that the full amount previously withdrawn must be paid back into your RRSP before the beginning of the given year in which you wish to participate a second time. Also, you must still qualify as a first-time home buyer. This applies for 1999 and subsequent years.

TAX TIP

Each spouse or common-law partner can withdraw eligible amounts under the home buyer's plan from any of their respective RRSPs, including spousal RRSPs. Also, each person can withdraw up to the $20,000 limit or $40,000 in aggregate (if purchasing the property jointly).

Persons with disabilities

If you are an existing home owner who has a disability or a relative of a person with a disability, you may withdraw funds from your RRSP under the home buyer's plan if the withdrawal is to assist you or your disabled relative to purchase a home.

Some conditions must be met first:

- You or your disabled relative must qualify for the "disability credit" (see article **74**).
- The home must be more accessible or better suited for your care or the care of your disabled relative.
- If you are not disabled, your disabled relative must live in the home or plan to occupy it within one year after the acquisition.

This provision applies to withdrawals in 1999 and subsequent years.

61 Using an RRSP to finance higher education

Since January 1, 1999, tax-free RRSP withdrawals can also be made to assist you in financing full-time training or education for you or your spouse or common-law partner. Withdrawals are limited to $10,000 per year, over a period of up to four calendar years, and subject to a cumulative total of $20,000.

To qualify, you or your spouse or common-law partner must be enrolled or committed to enroll as a full-time student in a qualifying education program of at least three months in duration at an eligible educational institution. The full-time criterion is dropped for disabled students.

Withdrawals must be repaid to the RRSP over a maximum 10-year period starting in the year after the last year that you or your spouse or common-law partner was enrolled as a full-time student. However, the repayments must commence no later than the sixth year after the initial withdrawal, even if full-time enrollment continues. If the required repayment is not made, an amount will have to be included in income. As with many tax situations, special rules apply.

62 Death and the RRSP

Should you die while you still own your RRSP, its entire value must be included in your income in the year of your death unless your spouse or common-law partner or your financially dependent children or grandchildren are entitled to the funds. Previously, a deduction could be claimed only for distributions to a financially dependent child or grandchild if you had no spouse at the time of death. However, for deaths occurring after 1998, a deduction can now be obtained for distributions to a financially dependent child or grandchild even where there is a surviving spouse or common-law partner. Therefore, if you designate your spouse or common-law partner or financially dependent child or grandchild as beneficiary of your RRSP, the proceeds from the plan will be taxable in your beneficiary's hands in the year in which they are received, unless they are transferred into his or her own tax-deferred plan.

If none of the above are designated as the beneficiary of your RRSP, its value may still be taxable in his or her hands upon your death, provided he or she is a beneficiary of your estate. This approach may provide more flexibility, but more paperwork will be involved.

For the purpose of these rules, a "financially dependent" child or grandchild is one whose income for the year preceding your death is less than the basic personal amount for the year (see **Table 1**). Other rules apply if you die after your plan has matured and you were receiving annuity payments from your RRSP or RRIF.

63 Retirement and the RRSP

Considering withdrawing funds from your RRSP? Then you should be aware of options available to you.

You are required to take the funds out of your RRSP by the end of the calendar year in which you reach the age of 69. When you collapse your RRSP, you may transfer the funds free of tax into a registered retirement income fund (RRIF) or a life or term annuity. The third option is to withdraw the funds and pay tax on the full amount. The choice will be based upon your retirement objectives, tax implications, and your cash flow requirements.

How RRIFs work

A RRIF provides you with varying amounts of income during retirement. If the payments are structured properly, a RRIF can continue indefinitely, essentially providing income for life. Payments from a RRIF are quite flexible. You can withdraw as much as you want, although you must take a minimum amount each year. Based on a specific formula, the minimum amount increases slightly each year as you age. RRIF payments are subject to tax in the year of receipt.

How annuities work

If your RRSP funds are transferred to an annuity, periodic payments from the annuity will also be taxed in the year of receipt. Annuities can be arranged to provide payments for either a fixed term (for example, to age 90) or for life. The main advantage to an annuity is that you can have some form of guarantee with respect to the amounts you will receive.

For instance, if you opt for a life annuity, you, or you and your spouse or common-law partner, can be guaranteed a specific income stream regardless of how long either of you survives. Nevertheless, an annuity is not as flexible as a RRIF. Once you purchase a life annuity and the funds are deposited and registered, they are locked in. You generally cannot de-register or cash in the plan at any time, or amend the terms of the contract.

Tax implications

If you withdraw funds from your RRSP, you will pay a withholding tax on the amount withdrawn. This will result in immediate taxation at your marginal tax rate. There are many options available to you when you decide to cash in your RRSP. Become familiar with the various alternatives and their tax consequences; that way, you'll be able to make an informed choice.

TAX TIP

Depending on your income, consider the pros and cons of withdrawing funds from your RRSP before you reach 65. The additional income will be subject to income tax at your marginal tax rate. However, if you receive income from your RRSP after you are 65, in addition to being taxed at your marginal tax rate, it may also reduce your eligibility at that time for the OAS benefit (see article **66**).

TAX TIP

If you need to withdraw funds from your RRSP, consider withdrawing the funds in increments of $5,000 or less to avoid the higher rate of withholding on larger amounts. However, keep in mind that any additional tax owing will still have to be paid when you file your tax return for the year.

64 Company pension plans

In general, if you are a member of a company pension plan, your RRSP contribution room is reduced by your pension adjustment (PA). As noted in article 52, this adjustment represents the present value of the pension benefits you earned for the previous year in your registered pension plan (RPP) or deferred profit sharing plan (DPSP).

There are two main types of RPPs: defined benefit plans, in which pension benefits are specified in the plan, and money purchase plans, in which pension benefits are based on combined employer/employee contributions plus earnings in the plan.

Defined benefit plans

As a member of a defined benefit plan, you are entitled to deduct 100% of all required contributions for current or post-1989 past service. You are also entitled to deduct a maximum of $3,500 per year for past-service contributions for service prior to 1990 while you were not a contributor to a pension plan, subject to an overall limit of $3,500 times the number of years of pre-1990 service bought back. This is in addition to any deduction for current or post-1989 service.

For years of pre-1990 service during which you were a contributor to the plan, the annual deduction is limited to $3,500 less the amount of other contributions deducted in the current year. This includes amounts for the current year, post-1989 past service, as well as pre-1990 past services while you were not a contributor. The $3,500 annual limit for deductibility of pre-1990 service contributions is disregarded in the year of death. You should consult with your tax adviser if you are subject to these complicated rules.

EXAMPLE

Defined benefit contribution

Assume you make a $4,000 contribution to your defined benefit plan in 2001 in respect of two years of service prior to 1990 while you were not a contributor to a pension plan. Your maximum deduction is $3,500 in 2001. The remaining $500 can be deducted in 2002.

Money purchase plans

You are entitled to deduct the amount you contributed to a money purchase plan during the year, subject to certain maximum amounts. For example, the maximum combined employer/employee contribution for 2001 is $13,500. Money purchase plans do not allow for past-service contributions.

The benefits you earn in your defined benefit pension plan, or total contributions to a money purchase plan, determine how much you can also contribute to your RRSP (see article **52**).

> If you leave a registered pension plan before retirement, you may be able to have your lost RRSP contribution room restored. The pension adjustment reversal is the mechanism designed to achieve this. Pension adjustment reversals will be added to the individual's RRSP contribution room for the year of termination (see article **52**).

Deferred profit sharing plans (DPSPs)

An alternative to the RPP is a deferred profit sharing plan (DPSP). Under this type of arrangement, your employer makes payments to a trustee who holds and invests the contributions for your benefit. However, unlike RPPs, employee contributions are not allowed.

The maximum contribution your employer can make on your behalf for 2001 is equal to the lesser of 18% of your earned income or $6,750. Similar to an RPP, employer contributions to a DPSP on your behalf reduce your RRSP contribution room (see article **52**).

65 Individual pension plans

Prior to 1991, employees who held at least 10% of their company's shares were not permitted to participate in the company's registered pension plan unless the value of benefits provided to non-shareholder employees was at least equal to the value of the benefits provided to themselves. However, since 1991, employees can now become members of a single-member pension plan, regardless of their share ownership.

What is an IPP?

The individual pension plan (IPP) is simply a defined benefit pension plan for one member. Subject to certain limitations, a defined benefit plan will provide for an annual pension equal to a percentage of your highest earnings over a given period. These plans can be either 100% funded by the employer or employer/employee funded. In general, you will not be able to fund more than 50% of the cost of the pension. In some cases, a well-designed IPP can provide greater tax assistance than an RRSP.

IPPs are not for everyone. The decision has to be an individual one based on several factors—your age, current and projected income level, the rate of return earned on the plan's assets, whether you are an owner-manager or an arm's-length executive, as well as several other considerations. Due to their complex nature, it is recommended that you consult with your tax adviser before investing in one of these plans.

66 Old Age Security clawback

The government imposes a special tax—the "clawback"—on your Old Age Security (OAS) payments if your net income for the year exceeds a certain annual threshold amount. For 2001, the threshold amount is $55,309. The amount of the clawback is equal to the lesser of your OAS payments or 15% of the amount by which your net income exceeds the threshold amount, and the clawback amounts are recovered through withholdings from your monthly OAS payments.

How it works

The reduction in the monthly payments for the period from January through June is based on your net income from two years ago. The reduction in the payments for July to December is based on your net income from last year.

Suppose your net income was $60,000 in 1999 and $62,000 in 2000. Your 1999 net income exceeded the threshold by $4,691, resulting in a projected OAS overpayment of $704 (15% × $4,691). Your payments for January 2001 through June 2001 are each reduced by $59 ($704 ÷ 12). Your 2000 net income exceeds the threshold by $6,691, resulting in a projected OAS overpayment of $1,004 (15% × $6,691). Your payments for July 2001 through December 2001 will each be reduced by $84 ($1,004 ÷ 12).

When you file your 2001 income tax return, the CCRA will calculate the actual OAS clawback based on your net income for the year. This amount will be compared to amounts withheld from monthly payments during the year. Any excess withheld will be refunded or applied against any other tax liability. Conversely, where the amount withheld falls short, you will be required to remit the difference.

TAX TIP

If you are just over the $55,309 clawback threshold, and your spouse or common-law partner's net income is below it, consider splitting your Canada Pension Plan (CPP) benefits with him or her if that will bring your net income below the limit (see article **93**).

TAX TIP

If you are considering making the election to include all of your spouse or common-law partner's taxable Canadian dividends in your income (see article **120**), ensure you are not subjecting yourself to the OAS clawback by using this strategy.

67 Childcare expenses

Work commitments may qualify you or your spouse (or other supporting individual) to deduct eligible expenses for childcare. Eligible costs include daycare or babysitting, boarding school, and certain camp expenses. Medical expenses, tuition, clothing, and transportation expenses are not eligible. You are also not allowed to deduct payments made to persons who are under 18 years of age and related to you. As with most qualifying expenses, there is a specified limit.

Who can claim?

In typical circumstances, where the child lives with both parents, the parent with the lower net income must claim the expense deduction. A parent with no income is considered to have the lower income and, therefore, will be the parent who is required to claim the expenses. The supporting parent with the higher income may only claim a deduction for that period during which the lower-income parent is infirm, confined to a bed or a wheelchair, attending a secondary school or a designated educational institution, or incarcerated in a correctional facility.

The amount that can be claimed for childcare is subject to special rules where the lower-income parent is in part-time attendance at a designated educational institution. Special rules also apply for single parents and parents who have separated during the year or are divorced.

How much can you deduct?

You can deduct up to $7,000 annually for each child who is six years of age or under at the end of the year and for each child who is dependent by reason of mental or physical infirmity. You can also deduct up to $4,000 for each child aged seven to 15 at any time in the year. This limit is increased to $10,000 annually for each child who is eligible for the disability tax credit (see article **74**). In general, the total deduction cannot exceed two-thirds of the salary or business income of the parent who is required to claim the deduction.

EXAMPLE

Deducting childcare expenses

You and your spouse are both employed and earn $30,000 and $65,000 per year, respectively. You incurred $10,000 in eligible childcare expenses in 2001 for your only child, a five-year-old. Since your income is less than your spouse's, you are the spouse entitled to deduct the childcare expenses. The maximum you can deduct is the lesser of $7,000 and two-thirds of your net income ($\frac{2}{3} \times \$30,000 = \$20,000$). Therefore, you can deduct $7,000 of childcare expenses in 2001.

68 Alimony and maintenance

Rules regarding alimony and maintenance payments changed significantly as of May 1, 1997. The main alteration is that child support payments are now treated very differently from spousal support payments. Periodic payments for spousal support continue to be taxable to the recipient and deductible by the payer, provided certain conditions are met.

What's changed?

For new or varied child support agreements made after April 30, 1997, the recipient will not pay tax on the payments and the payer will not receive a tax deduction for them.

The new rules also apply, in some situations, to older agreements and orders. A case in point is where a previous order or agreement is varied or amended after April 30, 1997, and results in a change in the amount of child support. In addition, parties to an agreement or order entered into before May 1, 1997, may jointly elect to have the new rules apply.

TAX TIP

If you are party to an agreement or order entered into before May 1, 1997, and you want the new rules to apply, you must jointly elect by filing form T1157. In some cases, you may also be required to file a copy of the agreement itself.

Registration of agreements

In some cases, you may be required to file form T1158, along with a copy of the agreement or court order, with the CCRA. Generally, these requirements extend to situations in which payments will continue to be deductible—for example, if an agreement is entered into after May 1, 1997, and it contains a requirement for either spousal payments only or for separate amounts for spousal and child support. Agreements entered into before May 1, 1997, may also have to be filed if they provide for spousal or spousal and child support payments and the agreement becomes subject to the new rules. Your tax adviser will be able to provide details on these filing requirements.

Child support payments from a resident of the United States are not taxable under the Canada-U.S. tax treaty.

Agreements or court orders prior to May 1, 1997

For the most part, the rules remain unchanged for alimony and maintenance payments made pursuant to a written separation agreement or court order in place before May 1, 1997. These amounts are deductible for tax purposes if they meet certain criteria. Also, if the taxpayer making the payments is allowed to deduct them, the taxpayer receiving the payments must include the amounts in income.

In general, to be deductible, the payments must be periodic, for the maintenance of your spouse and/or children, and pursuant to a written separation agreement or court order. Payments made in the same year before the agreement was signed (as well as those in the preceding year) may also be deductible, provided the agreement or court order recognizes these payments.

Support payments arising from the breakdown of a common-law relationship may also be deductible. The requirements for deductibility by the
payer and taxability to the recipient are similar to those discussed for separation or divorce, except that a court order (rather than a separation
agreement) is required.

Third-party rules

Rules have also been established regarding the tax treatment of alimony and
maintenance payments that have been paid to a third party rather than
directly to your spouse or former spouse. Such payments—which can
include medical bills, tuition fees, and mortgage payments—may qualify
for a deduction and corresponding income inclusion. To qualify, the expense
must have been incurred at a time when you and your spouse or former
spouse were separated and living apart, and such payments must have been
specifically provided for in the court order or written agreement.

69 The deductibility of legal fees during separation or divorce

The tax treatment of legal fees paid during a separation and divorce is a
confusing area. Although most of the legal fees incurred are non-
deductible—as a personal or living expense—legal fees incurred with
respect to support payments may be deductible. This will depend on
whether you are the payer or the recipient of such payments.

From the payer's standpoint, legal costs incurred in negotiating or
contesting an application for support payments are not deductible, nor
are any of the costs incurred to terminate or reduce the amount of such
payments. Legal expenses relating to custody or visitation rights are also
non-deductible.

From the recipient's standpoint, however, some or all of the legal fees
may be deductible—it depends on the circumstances.

Legal expenses incurred to obtain a lump-sum payment

Legal expenses incurred to obtain the payment of a lump-sum settlement
are generally not deductible unless the payment specifically relates to a
number of periodic child support payments that were in arrears.

Legal expenses incurred to obtain periodic support payments

The tax department recently changed its position on the deductibility of legal fees incurred to obtain periodic child support payments. Previously, legal fees incurred to establish a right to support amounts were not deductible, whereas legal fees incurred to enforce pre-existing rights were deductible. The department now permits the deduction of legal expenses incurred to establish a right to receive child support, even if the amount received does not have to be reported as income.

Legal fees incurred to establish the right to spousal support payments will continue to be non-deductible. However, fees incurred to enforce an existing spousal support order will be deductible.

Where legal fees incurred to obtain a divorce or separation include legal fees for child support, spousal support, custody, and/or visitation rights, the onus is on the taxpayer to establish the portion pertaining directly to obtaining maintenance for the child. Taxpayers in this situation should consider asking their lawyer to separately identify such costs on the invoice.

TAX TIP

If you have incurred legal fees as part of a separation or divorce, contact your tax adviser to determine whether any of the amounts are deductible. You may also be able to apply for a refund on fees paid in previous years.

70 The deductibility of other legal expenses

Most legal expenses are personal in nature and are not deductible. Legal costs paid to collect or establish a right to salary or wages from your employer or former employer are one exception to that rule. Legal expenses paid to collect or establish a right to a retiring allowance or pension benefit are also deductible within a seven-year carry-forward period. The deduction is limited to the amount of retiring allowance or pension benefits received, less any portion that has been transferred to an RPP or RRSP.

71 Moving expenses

If you moved from one location to another in Canada in 2001, you may qualify to deduct your eligible moving expenses on your 2001 return. You must have started work or carried on a business at your new location. In addition, your new residence must be at least 40 kilometres closer to your new work location, and a court case has concluded that this distance should be measured using the shortest normal route of travel open to the public.

Costs you can claim

Eligible moving expenses include travelling expenses incurred in connection with the move and the cost of transporting your household goods. The cost of meals and temporary accommodation for a period not exceeding 15 days is also eligible, as are the costs of selling your old residence or of breaking your lease if you were renting. Any loss you may incur on the sale of your former residence cannot be deducted.

And the federal government has recently expanded the list of eligible moving expenses to include mortgage interest, property taxes, insurance premiums, and payable costs—to a maximum of $5,000—associated with maintaining heat and power in a vacant former residence. This is in effect for a period that begins after 1997 and during which all reasonable efforts are made to sell the former residence. The costs of revising legal documents to reflect the taxpayer's new address, replacing drivers' licences and automobile permits, and having utilities connected and/or disconnected are also eligible for deduction. Again, these measures apply to expenses incurred after 1997.

Moving expenses paid by your employer cannot be claimed by you as a deduction. If your employer pays or reimburses you for part of your moving expenses, you may deduct all of your eligible moving expenses but must report the amounts paid by your employer as income. Eligible expenses are only deductible from the income earned at the new location. Amounts not deducted in the year of the move may be carried forward to the next year.

TAX TIP

Subject to the following comments, if you are moving to a new work location, any relocation payments should be clearly structured as a reimbursement of actual expenses incurred. Payments received as a blanket lump-sum allowance, rather than a reimbursement of costs already incurred, may leave you open to tax implications. Talk to your tax adviser about how the payments can be structured to avoid or minimize tax.

Amounts received from your employer

Numerous court cases have addressed the tax status of amounts received from your employer following relocation. Is the amount a non-taxable reimbursement or is it taxable? Due to the inconsistent court decisions and resulting uncertainty in this area, new rules were introduced in 1998 to provide that all subsidies paid directly or indirectly by an employer to help finance an employee's new or former residence will be taxable. One-half of amounts in excess of $15,000 paid directly or indirectly to an employee by an employer to compensate for a loss on the disposition of the former residence will also be taxable. If you began working in the new location before October, 1998, these new rules will apply to amounts provided or paid in 2001 and subsequent years. If you began working in the new location after September, 1998, the new rules applied at the time the benefit was received.

TAX TIP

If you have to start a job at a new location, but a permanent move to that area is not possible until the following year, you won't lose any of your eligible deductions because the two events do not coincide. That's because the courts are on your side. They have ruled that where a taxpayer commences employment at a new location but does not move until a subsequent year, the taxpayer has a right to claim moving expenses incurred in that subsequent year.

Student eligibility

Students can also claim moving expenses if they move to begin a job (including summer employment) or to start a business. If the move is to attend a full-time post-secondary institution, you can deduct the expenses, but only to the extent of your scholarship or research grant income.

Students' deductions

You live in Charlottetown and the University of British Columbia has offered you a $4,000 scholarship for the 2001 school year. You subsequently decide to attend full-time courses at that university and purchase an airline ticket for $1,200. Since the annual exemption limit for scholarship income is $3,000, you are subject to tax on $1,000 of the scholarship income. As a result, you will be able to deduct up to $1,000 of the cost of the airline ticket in 2001. If the amount is not claimed in 2001, you may be able to deduct it from scholarship or research grant income in 2002.

Optional method for claiming certain moving expenses

If you moved to a new work location in 2001, and would otherwise be entitled to claim moving expenses, you have the option of using a simplified method for claiming your meal and vehicle expenses.

Under the current detailed method, you must keep all related receipts and submit them upon request. Vehicle expenses include operating expenses—such as fuel, oil, tires, licence fees, insurance, maintenance, and repairs—and ownership expenses, such as depreciation (CCA), provincial tax, and financing charges.

Under this method, you also have to keep track of the kilometres you drove in that time period, as well as the kilometres you drove specifically for the purpose of moving. Your claim for vehicle expenses is the percentage of your total vehicle expenses that relate to the kilometres driven for moving expenses.

For example, if you drove 10,000 kilometres during the year, and 1,000 kilometres of that was related to your move, you can claim 1/10 of the total vehicle expenses on your tax return.

The new optional rules are as follows:

- Meal expenses: You can claim a flat rate of $11 a meal, to a maximum of $33 per day per person, without receipts.
- Vehicle expenses: This method involves the use of various pre-established flat rates. If you choose this option, you do not need to keep receipts. Instead, you simply keep track of the kilometres you

drove during the tax year for your trips relating to the move. To determine the amount you can claim, multiply the number of kilometres by the cents-per-kilometre rate from the chart below for the province or territory from which the travel begins. The current provincial rates, which are subject to change, are as follows:

Saskatchewan	36
Alberta	37.5
Prince Edward Island	38.5
Nova Scotia	39.5
New Brunswick	39.5
Manitoba	39
British Columbia	41
Ontario	40.5
Newfoundland	40.5
Quebec	43.5
Northwest Territories, Yukon, and Nunavut	44

For example, if you moved from Ottawa to Montreal, you would have travelled about 200 kilometres. Your vehicle expense claim would be 200 kilometres, multiplied by the rate of 40.5¢ for Ontario, for a total of $81.

This simplified option is available for 1999 and subsequent years.

72 What is a tax credit?

Several of the articles that follow refer to a tax credit. Although there is a substantial difference between a tax credit and a tax deduction, it is easy to confuse the two. Items that are deductible reduce your taxable income, with the actual amount of tax saved depending on your personal tax rate. If you are in the highest tax bracket, the deduction is generally worth anywhere from 39¢ to 49¢ on the dollar (depending on your province of residence—see **Table 3**). If you are in the lowest bracket, it is generally worth around 25¢ on the dollar (again, depending on your province of residence). If you have no taxable income, a deduction may not save you any tax at all.

A tax credit, on the other hand, is a deduction from tax owing. Provided the credit can be used, each taxpayer receives the same tax relief from a tax credit, regardless of his or her particular tax bracket.

Before the year 2000, in all provinces except Quebec, personal income tax was calculated as a percentage of basic federal tax. Most tax credits that reduced federal tax also reduced the applicable provincial tax. Therefore, to calculate the real value of a tax credit, you also had to include the provincial saving. Starting in 2000, some of the provinces opted to use taxable income rather than basic federal tax as their assessment base. The rest of the other provinces followed suit in 2001. As a result, those provinces using the "tax on income" system now have the option of either following the federal tax credit system or introducing tax credits that will be unique to their particular province. Due to the changes to the provincial tax systems, the sections that follow that refer to tax credits will generally just comment on the federal tax credit. The provincial tax credits may or may not parallel the treatment provided at the federal level.

EXAMPLE
_____

What they are worth

Assume you live in Ontario and you are in the highest tax bracket (29%). Your combined federal and provincial marginal tax rate in 2001 is 46.41% (see **Table 3**). A $100 tax deduction will save you $46.41 in tax. Your tax savings will be reduced where you are in a lower tax bracket.

Most federal tax credits are calculated using the lowest federal rate of tax (16%). Therefore, if you have an amount of $100 that is eligible for a tax credit, you will save $16 in federal income tax. The same amount will result in an Ontario tax credit of $6.20. Therefore, the combined tax savings are $22.20—regardless of your tax bracket.

73 Federal personal tax credits

Federal personal tax credits are calculated as 16% of specified "personal amounts" (see **Table 1**) and are allowed as a deduction in computing your federal tax liability.

You may claim personal exemption credits for yourself, your spouse or common-law partner, and certain other persons who are related to you by blood, marriage, or adoption. Income earned by your spouse or common-law partner or other dependants may reduce the amount you are entitled to claim. With the exception of the equivalent-to-married credit, a general dependant tax credit cannot be claimed for children under 19. However, an amount can be claimed for an infirm dependant who is 18 years of age or older at the end of the year (see below).

In 2000, full indexation was restored to the personal tax system. The factor effective for January 1, 2001, is 2.5%.

Basic Personal Credit

For 2001, everyone is entitled to claim a basic personal amount of $7,412. This equates to a federal personal tax credit of $1,186.

The married credit

You may claim a credit for the married amount if at any time in the year you were married or had a common-law partner (see articles **84** and **85**) and you were not living separate and apart because of a breakdown of the relationship. For 2001, the married amount is $6,294. This equates to a married credit of $1,007 (16% × $6,294). The married amount is reduced on a dollar-for-dollar basis by the dependant's income in excess of $629.

The equivalent-to-married credit

If at any time during the year you were unmarried or separated from your spouse or common-law partner, you may be entitled to claim a personal tax credit known as the equivalent-to-married credit. To qualify, you must have maintained a home in which you and your qualifying dependant lived. As well, your dependant must be related to you and dependent on you for support. Other qualifying factors include that the dependant is either under 18 years of age at any time during 2001, your parent or grandparent, or mentally or physically infirm. Two or more supporting relatives cannot split this tax credit. The equivalent-to-married credit is computed on the same basis as the married credit.

The infirm dependant credit

You may claim a dependant tax credit for a relative who is 18 or older before the end of the year if the individual is dependent on you because of mental or physical infirmity at any time in the year. Unlike the credits above, it is not necessary that the dependant cohabit with you, nor does the disability have to be severe enough that the dependant qualifies for the disability tax credit (see article **74**). The CCRA's position is that the dependency must be brought about solely by reason of the infirmity, and the infirmity must be such that it requires the person to be dependent on the individual for a considerable period of time.

For 2001, this credit is increased to $3,500. This equates to a federal credit of $560 (16% × $3,500). The infirm dependant amount is reduced on a dollar-for-dollar basis by the dependant's income in excess of $4,966.

The caregiver credit

Because of the above income threshold, most taxpayers who provide care to an elderly relative living with them cannot claim the above credit because payments under the Old Age Security and the guaranteed income supplement programs are well in excess of this amount. As a result, beginning in 1998 and in subsequent years, there is another tax credit available if you reside with and provide in-home care for a parent or grandparent who is 65 or over. The age restriction is removed if the relative is dependent on you by reason of mental or physical infirmity.

Like to the infirm dependant credit, the maximum credit will reduce federal taxes by $560. The major difference is the net income threshold at which the credit begins to be reduced. For 2001, the dependant's threshold is $11,953. No credit will be available if the dependant's income exceeds $15,453. And no credit will be available if any person claims an equivalent-to-married or infirm dependant tax credit in respect of the dependant.

74 Disability credit

Individuals suffering from severe and prolonged mental or physical impairment can obtain an additional federal credit of $960 (16% × $6,000) and, if the disabled person is a child under 18, there is an additional supplement that results in a federal credit of $1,520 (16% × $9,500).

To qualify, a doctor must certify on form T2201 that there exists a severe and prolonged impairment that "markedly restricts" the individual's activities of daily living. The impairment must have lasted, or can reasonably be expected to last, for a continuous period of 12 months. Once obtained, the form continues to be valid until the cessation date noted on the form or until there is a change in condition. There is no requirement to file a new certificate each year. Recent changes have extended eligibility for the disability tax credit to individuals who would be markedly restricted but for therapy administered to them at least three times each week for a total duration averaging not less than 14 hours a week in order to sustain one of their vital functions—for example, individuals on kidney dialysis and cystic fibrosis sufferers.

Those making a new application for this credit will find that the tax department will review the claim to determine eligibility before assessing the tax return. For this reason, if you are claiming the disability credit for the first time, you must paper file your return. Once approved, this amount will be able to be claimed as long as circumstances do not change.

Transferring the credit

If you cannot take advantage of this credit, it can be transferred to your spouse or common-law partner or other supporting person. The list of relatives who can claim a person's unused disability tax credit has recently been expanded to include a brother, sister, aunt, uncle, nephew, or niece.

However, no claim may be made under this provision if a medical expense credit has been claimed by you or anyone on your behalf for costs relating to a full-time attendant or nursing home care. On the other hand, you may claim the attendant care deduction (see article **78**) and the disability credit at the same time, as long as no additional attendant or nursing home claim has been made on your behalf. To confuse things even further, the disability tax credit can also be claimed where an amount is claimed as a medical expense for attendant care (to a maximum amount of $10,000 per year).

TAX TIP

If you or anyone else paid for an attendant or for care in a nursing home or other establishment because of your impairment, it may be beneficial to claim the amounts paid as medical expenses instead of the disability amount. In some circumstances, both may be claimed.

The rules relating to this area of credits are exceedingly complex and often confusing. It is recommended that you have a tax adviser analyze your particular circumstances before you file a return to come up with the appropriate claim or combination of claims that make sound economic sense.

75 Tax credits for charitable donations

Donations to registered charities, registered Canadian amateur athletic associations, Canadian municipalities, the federal government, or a provincial government are eligible for a tax credit that reduces the taxes you have to pay. As a general rule, donations to U.S. charitable organizations qualify for the credit, provided you also have U.S. source net income that is taxable in Canada.

Without exception, donations may be claimed only after they are paid—pledges don't count. Unused claims may be carried forward for up to five years and donations made in the year of death may be carried back one year.

The general annual limit on charitable donations is now 75% of net income. However, the limit on gifts by individuals in the year of death (and prior year) is 100%.

Save those receipts

To secure the credit, you must include the original official receipts issued by the registered charity or association with your tax return. These receipts will include the registration number of the given institution. Photocopies of receipts are not acceptable, and filing cancelled cheques is not sufficient either. If you are filing your return electronically (see article 137) or by NETFILE or TELEFILE (see article 138), you are not required to file these receipts with your return, but you must retain them for future audit purposes.

The credit is 16% on the first $200 of donations claimed in the year, and 29% on the amount in excess of $200. After factoring in provincial tax savings, donations in excess of $200 will save you anywhere from 39% to 50% (depending on your province of residence).

TAX TIP

If you and your spouse or common-law partner donate more than $200 in any one year, the tax credit will be larger if one of you claims the entire amount. That way, there is only the one $200 amount to be credited at 16%, instead of two claims.

EXAMPLE

Joining forces

Suppose you donated $400 in 2001 and your spouse donated $600. Rather than claim individually, where each of you receives a 16% credit on the first $200, you should pool the amounts and have one of you claim it. That way, you receive a 16% credit on $200 and a 29% credit on $800.

Donating property

If you donate capital property to a registered charity, you can elect to value the gift at any amount up to its fair market value. The amount that is claimed as a donation must also be reported as your proceeds of disposition of the property.

To account for the fact that the disposition may result in taxable income to the donor, the general annual limit of 75% of net income is increased to effectively allow 100% of the donor's taxable income created by the disposition to be offset by tax credits. In addition, donors of depreciable assets, such as buildings and equipment, will be entitled to increase the net income limit for such a donation to ensure that the donor has enough tax credits to more than offset the tax arising from both the recaptured depreciation and taxable capital gain.

If you donate "eligible property" to a charity, you are entitled to additional tax relief. If you donate such property to a charity (other than a private charitable foundation) after February 18, 1997, and before 2002, the income inclusion rate is reduced by one-half, i.e., to 25% for donations after October 17, 2000. Eligible property includes securities, such as shares and bonds listed on a prescribed stock exchange, as well as mutual fund units.

EXAMPLE
Sharing the wealth

It is November, 2001. Your net income for 2001 is expected to be $125,000, and despite talk of mergers (or maybe because of it), you decide to donate all of your bank shares, with a fair market value of $100,000, to a registered charity. When you purchased the shares in 1990, they cost $10,000, and now this results in a $90,000 capital gain. Your 2001 net income? Here's the outcome:

Net income	$125,000
Taxable capital gain (25% × $90,000)	22,500
Total Net Income	$147,500

The donation amount eligible for tax credit is
   calculated as follows:

75% of net income	$110,625
25% of taxable capital gain	5,625
Limit	$116,250

Available for credit (donation amount)	$100,000

Assuming your marginal tax rate is 45%, the tax saving
   arising from the donation is:

Tax on the taxable capital gain (45% × $22,500)	$ 10,125
Tax savings from donation credit (45% × $100,000)	45,000
Overall tax savings	34,875

The $10,125 tax liability arising from the donation of the property is more than offset by the $45,000 tax savings arising from the donation.

TAX TIP

With the increases in donation limits, it is generally no longer necessary to elect proceeds at an amount lower than the fair market value of the property to eliminate a current tax liability arising from the donation.

Taxpayers, including artists, who donate their works of art to a charity, public art gallery, or other public institution may qualify for special tax treatment.

Gift of stock option shares

Special rules come into play if you gift stock option shares to a qualifying charity.

If the stock option benefit with respect to the share has been deferred (see article **34**), you have to include a taxable benefit in income at the time the share is donated to the charity. If the share does not qualify for the deferral, the benefit is included in income at the time the option is exercised. If certain conditions are met, you can claim a deduction from income that will effectively tax the employment benefit at the same rate as a capital gain (see article **111**).

If shares acquired under a stock option agreement are donated to a charity, there is an additional deduction that will reduce the net income inclusion by one-half—similar to the tax treatment given to other public securities. Again, to qualify for this additional deduction, certain conditions must be met and you must donate the shares in the year in which they are acquired and within 30 days of their acquisition. This deduction applies to securities donated before 2002.

Other gifts

Donations do not always have to be in the form of money or tangible property. The donation of a life insurance policy to a registered charitable organization qualifies for the credit (see article **107**), provided certain conditions are met. The amount eligible for the credit is the cash surrender value of the policy and any accumulated dividends and interest at the time of the transfer. Under certain conditions, the gift of a residual interest in a trust or estate may also qualify for the credit. Your tax adviser can provide additional information in these areas.

Charitable gifts made on the death of an individual may qualify for the charitable donation tax credit in the year of death and prior year. Effective for deaths occurring after 1998, the charitable donation tax credit is extended to donations of RRSP, RRIF, and insurance proceeds that are made pursuant to a direct beneficiary designation. Previously, the tax credit was only available where the amounts were donated under the individual's will, in which case the amount donated was subject to probate.

Art donations

For computing capital gains, the adjusted cost base and proceeds of disposition of personal-use property are both deemed to be at least $1,000 (see article **90**). However, this rule will not apply if property was acquired after February 27, 2000, as part of an arrangement in which the property is donated as a charitable gift.

This measure is intended to ensure that small donations will be subject to tax on capital gains if the donation value exceeds the donor's cost and is primarily aimed at the arrangements for donating art that have been marketed recently. In addition to this rule, there is another that could assess a civil penalty against the promoter of the arrangement for art if it includes a false statement or omission that may be used for tax purposes by another person (see article **146**).

76 Political donations

Contributions to registered political parties generate tax credits (within limits), not tax deductions. Political contributions to federal parties can only be applied against federal income taxes.

For 2001, the credit is calculated as follows: 75% of the first $200, 50% on the next $350, and 33⅓% of any contribution over $550. The maximum credit allowed in any one year is $500, which means that you don't receive credit for political contributions over $1,075. Some provinces provide similar credits against provincial income taxes for contributions made to provincial political parties. To claim the credit, you must attach a copy of the receipt to your return.

For both federal and provincial purposes, the credit may reduce only taxes paid or payable. If you are not liable for any taxes in 2001, the credit is lost. It cannot be carried forward to 2002.

Consider spreading your political contributions over two years. For example, if you contribute $700 in 2001, your federal tax credit will be $375. If instead you contribute $350 in 2001 and $350 in 2002, your political contribution tax credit will be $225 each year, for a total of $450.

77 Medical expenses

Medical expenses paid within any 12-month period ending in the year are eligible for a tax credit claim. Expenses reimbursed by either your employer or a private or government-sponsored health care plan are not allowed. The list of eligible expenses is extensive and includes fees paid to a private health or dental plan. You may claim medical expenses for yourself, your spouse or common-law partner, and certain related persons.

The legal representatives of a deceased taxpayer may claim any medical expenses paid—for the year of death—by the taxpayer or his legal representative within any 24-month period that includes the date of death. The same expense may not be claimed more than once.

For 2001, total eligible medical expenses must first be reduced by the lesser of two amounts—3% of your net income or $1,678. The tax credit is 16% of the amount remaining.

Select your 12-month period to maximize the tax credit. The 12-month period ending in the year may be varied from year to year, but you cannot claim the same expense twice. Keep your receipts for next year if some of your 2001 expenses are not claimed as a credit in 2001.

A refundable medical expense supplement is also available to eligible individuals who have business or employment income of at least $2,598. The refundable credit is 25% of medical expenses that qualify for the regular medical expense tax credit, up to a maximum of $520. However, it is reduced by 5% of the taxpayer's (and spouse or common-law partner's) income in excess of $18,106. This credit is in addition to the tax credit for medical expenses.

78 Attendant for a disabled person

Disabled persons who incur costs for attendant care that allows the earning of income can deduct these expenses. The deduction is limited to two-thirds of "earned income," which is basically salary and business income.

As an alternative, you can claim the cost of attendant care incurred as a medical expense (see article **77**) even if you are not earning income. The amount eligible for tax credit is $10,000 ($20,000 in the year of death).

TAX TIP

If you are disabled and your income is over $30,000, the deduction for attendant care is worth more to you than claiming the medical expense tax credit. You will be further ahead economically by taking the deduction.

This deduction can also be claimed by persons who require an attendant in order to attend school. In general, this deduction is limited to $375 times the number of weeks of attendance at the institution or school

79 Tuition fees and education credits

Students are entitled to a tax credit equal to 16% of tuition fees at qualifying educational and training institutions. They are also entitled to an education credit of 16% of $400 per month (or $64) for the number of months in the year in which they were full-time students. This includes full-time post-secondary students enrolled in correspondence courses.

To assist part-time students, there is an education credit equal to 16% of $120 per month of part-time attendance at a Canadian educational institution. To qualify, the student must be enrolled in an eligible program of at least three consecutive weeks' duration, with a minimum of 12 course hours each month.

What's covered?

Qualifying fees include those for attending a Canadian university, college, or other educational institution providing courses at a post-secondary level. If you attend a primary or secondary school that provides courses at the post-secondary level, you may also qualify for the tuition credit if the course paid for is at the post-secondary level. Courses you take to improve or obtain an occupational skill also qualify, provided the institution is certified by the Minister of Human Resources Development. To qualify for the tuition credit, the total fees paid to each institution for the year must be at least $100. Subject to certain restrictions, tuition fees paid to universities outside Canada also qualify for the credit.

Both the tuition fee credit and the education credit are claimed on a calendar-year basis. All claims for tuition fee credits must be supported by formal receipts. Claims for the $400-per-month education credit must be supported by form T2202 or T2202A, which is completed by the educational institution you attend. Currently, you do not have to file these supporting documents with your return, but they must be available if requested by the tax department.

TAX TIP

If you cannot fully utilize your tuition and education tax credits to reduce taxes payable to zero, all or a portion of the unused credits may be transferred to a spouse or common-law partner or supporting parent or grandparent.

Should a student be unable to use all or a portion of a credit, he or she can transfer up to $5,000 of it to an eligible person, which translates into an $800 federal tax credit. To make this designation, the student must complete and sign form T2202. A copy of the signed form should be kept by the designated person and, if applicable, by the student to support the amount claimed. Currently, the form does not need to be filed with the return but must be available if requested by the CCRA.

Prior to 1997, tax credits earned for tuition fees and the education amount were lost if not used by the student or a person to whom they can be transferred. Beginning with credits earned in 1997, students are entitled to carry forward unused tuition and education credits indefinitely. This will allow students to utilize the credit when they have enough income. Any amount not used in the current year by the student and not transferred to an eligible person will be automatically available to carry forward. Transfer to an eligible person will continue to be restricted to $5,000 and will be available for credits earned in the current year only.

TAX TIP

Students must provide all necessary information to the CCRA to establish the carry-forward. This will require filing an income tax return even if one is not otherwise required.

80 Claiming your spouse or common-law partner's unused credits

TAX TIP

Does your spouse or common-law partner (see articles **84** and **85**) have so little taxable income that he or she cannot use all of the federal tax credits to which he or she is entitled? Then you are in a position to claim the portion of the qualifying credits that he or she is unable to use. However, you may not receive a transfer of credits from your spouse or common-law partner if you were separated at the end of the year and for a 90-day period that began at any time in the year. Unused credits that can be transferred include the tuition fee and education credits (see article **79**), the pension credit (see article **81**), the disability credit (see article **74**), and the age credit (see article **82**).

To determine how much your spouse or common-law partner can transfer to you, you must calculate his or her federal tax liability before applying any of these credits. Then, you subtract from this amount his or her basic personal tax credit (see article **73** and **Table 1**), and the amount of any tax credits arising from EI or CPP contributions. If there are no federal taxes payable after applying these three credits, then the full amount of his or her unused credits can be transferred to you. If your spouse or common-law partner still owes federal tax after deducting these credits (basic, EI, and CPP), the qualifying credits must be applied first to eliminate his or her remaining federal tax liability. The remaining portion can be transferred to you.

EXAMPLE

To your credit

Suppose you earn $100,000 of employment income and your spouse earns $8,000 of interest income in 2001. As well, your spouse attended university full-time for four months and paid $2,500 in tuition fees.

Your spouse would have taxable income of $8,000 and an eligible tuition and education amount of $3,300 [$2,500 + (4 × $200)]. The amount of credits transferable to you is calculated as follows:

Spouse's Tax Liability:	
Taxable income	$8,000
	16%
Federal tax (before tax credits)	1,280
Personal tax credit	1,186
Federal tax (before tuition credit)	94
Tuition credit needed to reduce	
taxes payable to zero	(94)
Federal tax	0

As shown above, your spouse must use a portion of the tuition and education credit to eliminate his or her federal tax liability. The remaining tuition and education amount of $2,713 [$3,300 − ($94 ÷ 16%)] is eligible for transfer to your 2001 tax return.

81 Pension credit

A tax credit is available for up to $1,000 of pension income. The eligible amounts differ depending on whether you were 65 or older in the year. For those under 65 as of December 31, 2001, "qualifying pension income" includes life annuity payments out of a superannuation or pension plan and certain payments received as a result of the death of a spouse or common-law partner.

If you were 65 or older in 2001, other defined payments such as annuity payments out of your RRSP or RRIF also qualify for the pension credit. Qualifying pension income does not include CPP, OAS, or guaranteed income supplement payments.

TAX TIP

If you do not already benefit from the pension income tax credit, and you are 65 years of age or over, consider creating pension income by purchasing an annuity that yields $1,000 of interest income annually. Alternatively, you can use some of the funds in your RRSP to purchase an annuity or RRIF to provide you with $1,000 of annual pension income.

82 Age credit

Canadian taxpayers 65 or older are entitled to a federal tax credit of $579, calculated as 16% of the "age amount," currently at $3,619. This credit is one of those credits that can be transferred between spouses or common-law partners (see article **80**). It is reduced at a rate of 15% to the extent a taxpayer's income exceeds a prescribed threshold amount, currently at $26,941, and it is fully eliminated once income exceeds $51,068.

TAX TIP

Are you able to manage your income level, but require more than $26,941 per year on average? Then you may find it beneficial to receive larger amounts of income in one year and a reduced amount in the next. This will ensure that the age credit amount is reduced in only one year. Similarly, this strategy may reduce the total Old Age Security clawback (see article **66**).

83 Canada child tax benefit

It's been several years now since the family allowance, the non-refundable tax credit for children under age 18, and the refundable child tax credit were all replaced by the Canada child tax benefit (CCTB) system.

How it works

A monthly payment is issued to those who qualify, and each payment is based on the prior year's combined income of you and your spouse or common-law partner. Payments for the first six months of the year are based on net income from two years ago, and payments for the next six months are based on net income from last year. The payments under this system are not taxable.

For the year 2001, the CCTB basic benefit will be reduced if combined incomes exceed $30,754 and the supplement will be reduced if the combined incomes exceed $21,744. These income thresholds will increase in July 2002.

To qualify for this new program and receive child benefit payments, you and your spouse must each file an income tax return.

84 Taxation of common-law couples

Common-law couples are treated the same as legally married couples for all provisions of the Income Tax Act. A "common-law partner" is defined as a person who has lived with you in a conjugal relationship for at least one year or who is the natural or adoptive parent of your child. Commencing in 2001, a common-law partner also includes a same-sex partner (see article **85**). As a result, common-law couples are:

- able to claim the married credit,
- permitted to contribute to spousal RRSPs,
- required to combine their incomes to determine entitlement to the GST/HST credit and the child tax benefit,
- subject to the income attribution rules,
- allowed to transfer assets to a surviving partner on a tax-deferred basis upon the death of the other partner, and
- subject to all other income tax provisions that formerly applied only to married persons.

85 Taxation of same-sex common-law couples

New legislation has recently been introduced to treat same-sex common-law couples the same as other couples for all purposes of the Income Tax Act. Same-sex common-law couples are now eligible for the same tax benefits, and subject to the same obligations, as married couples and opposite-sex common-law partners (see article **84**).

These changes are effective for the 2001 and subsequent taxation years. However, as a transitional measure, same-sex common-law partners were permitted to jointly elect to be treated as common-law partners for the 1998, 1999, or 2000 tax year. If you wanted this new rule to apply to one of these prior years, you had to request it in writing by the due date for filing your 2000 tax return—either April 30, 2001, or June 15, 2001. An election made for a prior year established your status for all subsequent years. For example, if an election was made for the 1998 tax year, that election also applied to 1999 and 2000.

TAX TIP

If you reside with a same-sex common-law partner, contact your tax adviser to determine how these new rules will affect your tax situation.

86 Special rules for artists and entertainers

Artists and entertainers are entitled to special treatment under the Income Tax Act.

If you are employed as a musician, and required to provide a musical instrument as a condition of your employment, you may deduct the cost of maintenance, rent or capital cost allowance (see article 7), and insurance for the instrument. The amount deducted for musical instrument costs cannot exceed the income from employment as a musician, after you deduct all other employment expenses.

Artists and entertainers receiving employment income are entitled to deduct related expenses actually incurred, up to a maximum of 20% of such income but not more than $1,000. This deduction is in addition to the deductions all employees may be entitled to for most other expenses, such as automobile and related travelling expenses. However, it is reduced by the sum of the amounts claimed for interest and capital cost allowance on an automobile and for musical instrument costs (see above).

TAX TIP

Expenses incurred in the year, but restricted by the 20% or $1,000 limit, may be carried forward indefinitely. Don't overlook these carry-forward balances when calculating your income from artistic employment.

87 Special rules for the clergy

If you are a member of the clergy, you may be able to claim a deduction in respect of your residence. This deduction recognizes that your personal residence often serves as an office or meeting place for members of your congregation or parish. The amount of the deduction depends on whether or not your employer provides the residence or you provide it yourself.

Where your employer provides you with living accommodations, you can deduct the value of the accommodation to the extent that it is included in your employment income.

Effective for 2001 and subsequent years, where you provide your own living accommodations, you can claim a deduction equal to the least of the following three amounts:

a) your total remuneration from the office or employment;
b) ⅓ of that total remuneration or $10,000, whichever is greater; or
c) the fair rental value of your residence (or an amount equal to the fair rental value of your residence, if owned).

The calculation is adjusted if you are only employed as clergy for part of the year or if other amounts are claimed as a deduction in respect of the same accommodation.

In addition, if you want to claim the clergy residence deduction, you must file a prescribed form signed by your employer with your income tax return to the effect that you qualify to claim this deduction.

88 Taxation of emergency volunteers

This article will be of interest to you if you receive money from a government, municipality, or other public authority as an emergency worker: as a volunteer ambulance technician, fire fighter, or in some other emergency capacity.

The first $1,000 of remuneration is now exempt from tax. Only amounts over and above this $1,000 amount should be reported on your T4. For example, if you receive $2,500 in 2001 as a volunteer fire fighter, your T4 should only report total remuneration of $1,500.

However, if you were employed by the same authority for work other than as a volunteer, for the same or similar duties, this $1,000 exemption is not available.

89 Principal residence rules

Your "principal residence" is generally any residential property owned and occupied by you or your spouse or common-law partner, your former spouse or common-law partner, or your child at any time in the year. It can be a house, condominium, cottage, mobile home, trailer, or even a live-aboard boat, and it need not be located in Canada. Any gain on the sale of a principal residence is tax-free. However, if you sell your principal residence, you should be aware that some tax rules apply.

Just because you live in a house that you own does not automatically qualify it as a principal residence. For example, building contractors or house renovators who follow a pattern of living for a short period of time in a home they have built or renovated and then selling it at a profit may be subject to tax on their gains as ordinary business income.

Designating a principal residence

A home can be designated as your principal residence for each year in which you, your spouse or common-law partner, and/or your children were residents in Canada and ordinarily lived in it for some time during the particular year. You are allowed to designate only one home as your principal residence for a particular year. If you are unable to designate your home as your principal residence for all the years you owned it, a portion of any gain on sale may be subject to tax as a capital gain. The portion of the gain subject to tax is based upon a formula that takes into account the number of years you owned the home and the number of years it was designated as your principal residence.

Suppose you and your spouse own two residences, perhaps a home in the city and a cottage out of town. Only one of these homes can be designated as your family's principal residence each year. Before 1982, each spouse could designate a separate property as a principal residence for a particular year, provided the property was not jointly owned. However, for each year after 1981, the rules have tightened up and couples cannot designate more than one home in total as their principal residence each year.

To help you make this designation, you should determine the fair market value of both homes as of December 31, 1981. Factors to consider will include the relative appreciation of each house and the expected timing of any sale.

Tax issues

If you made a capital gains election on property designated as a principal residence (see article 112), the tax implications on the eventual disposition of the property will depend on a number of factors. They include the value of the property at the time of disposition, the number of years it was designated as a principal residence at the time of making the capital gains election, and the years it is designated as a principal residence after 1994. A property may still be designated as a principal residence on disposition even if it was not designated as such at the time of making the election. The benefit of the election may, however, be reduced. The rules in this area are quite complex and well worth a trip to your tax adviser's office.

TAX TIP

Be careful before designating a foreign-owned home as your principal residence. Even though the gain under Canadian rules is tax-free, you may incur a foreign tax liability when you sell your home.

Homes for rent

If you move out and rent your home, you can continue to treat the house as your principal residence for four additional years, or possibly more. There are also rules that apply if you own property to earn rental income and subsequently convert the property to personal use. Basically, at the time of the change in use, you are deemed to have disposed of the property at its fair market value. If this value exceeds your original cost, you will have to report a capital gain. However, you can make a special election to defer recognizing this gain until you ultimately sell the home. This election is not available if you have claimed depreciation on the property for any year after 1984.

TAX TIP

Contemplating renting out your home or converting a rental property to personal use? Another good reason to visit your tax adviser.

90 Selling personal-use capital property

Profits from the sale of almost all capital assets, with the exception of your principal residence, are subject to tax as a capital gain. Unfortunately, losses from the sale of most personal capital assets are not deductible.

What's involved

If you sell your boat or your car at a loss, you cannot claim it as a capital loss. But if you sell at a profit, one-half of the gain is taxable (three-quarters for dispositions before February 28, 2000, and two-thirds for dispositions between February 28 and October 17, 2000—see article 111). With the exception of certain donations of art (see article 75), assets that have a cost of $1,000 or less and are sold for $1,000 or less are exempt from this rule. But don't start preparing that For Sale ad just yet—assets that cost less than $1,000 but are sold for more than $1,000 still face a tax bill on the difference between their sale price and the cutoff point of $1,000.

When a capital gains election was made on a personal-use property (see article 112), the cost base of the asset is generally the amount designated in the election. When the asset is sold, the difference between the sale price and the amount elected is a capital gain.

Losses from the sale of certain types of personal property, referred to as "listed personal property," can be applied against gains from the sale of such property. Listed personal property includes coins, stamps, jewellery, rare books, paintings or sculptures, and other similar works of art. Losses on listed personal property can be carried back three years and forward seven years, but they can only be applied against gains from the sale of similar property.

EXAMPLE

Buying and selling

In 1996, you purchased a painting (which is listed personal property) at a cost of $2,000, and a boat (which is personal-use property) at a cost of $3,500. Five years later, in 2001, you sold both items for $3,000 each. The sale of the painting will result in a capital gain of $1,000 ($3,000 − $2,000) to be reported on your 2001 tax return.

The sale of the boat triggered a capital loss of $500 ($3,000 − $3,500), which cannot be claimed because it is personal-use property and not listed personal property.

However, if the asset in question were a diamond necklace instead of a boat (assuming the same cost and sale price), the capital loss may be applied against the gain on the painting, resulting in a net capital gain of $500 being reported on your 2001 tax return.

91 Transfers or loans to spouses or common-law partners and family members

All capital properties, such as shares in companies and real estate, are automatically transferred between spouses or common-law partners on a tax-free basis. If you want the transfer to take place at fair market value, you must file a special election requesting this treatment when you file your tax return for the year of the transfer. If such an election is filed, you will report a capital gain (assuming the property has appreciated in value), and the property's tax cost to your spouse or common-law partner will increase accordingly.

Selling the property

When the property is eventually sold by your spouse or common-law partner to a third party, you will have to report any capital gain realized on the sale unless the following very specific requirements have been met. First, your spouse or common-law partner must have paid fair market value for the property at the time of the transfer. You must also have made the fair market value election (as noted above), and sufficient annual interest on any unpaid purchase price must have been paid in full no later than January 30 of the following year. Provided these conditions have been met, any subsequent capital gain realized on a sale to a third party will be taxed in your spouse or common-law partner's hands.

EXAMPLE
Sharing the wealth

A benevolent mood comes over you and you decide to transfer your shares of XYZ Co. to your spouse. You acquired the shares in 1994 at a cost of $1,000 and they have a current fair market value of $5,000. For tax purposes, your spouse will be deemed to have acquired the shares from you for $1,000. Therefore, you will not recognize a capital gain or loss on the transfer. However, you will be taxed on any capital gain arising when your spouse disposes of the shares and the gain will be calculated using your original cost of $1,000.

Alternatively, by attaching a note to your tax return, you may elect to have the transfer take place at fair market value. As a result of making this election, you will report a capital gain of $4,000 and your spouse will be deemed to have acquired the shares from you at a cost of $5,000.

Now, assume you have made this election and your spouse subsequently sells the shares for $6,000. If your spouse did not pay you fair market value for the shares, the resulting capital gain of $1,000 is taxable in your hands. However, if your spouse paid you $5,000 for the shares, say by way of a loan from you, the $1,000 gain would be taxable in your spouse's hands—provided your spouse pays a reasonable rate of annual interest on the loan within the required time period.

Special rules apply where the property has been transferred between spouses or common-law partners as part of a property settlement or where the couple is separated at the time of sale to a third party.

Transfers to other family members

A transfer of capital property to other family members is taxed just as if you sold the property at its fair market value. If the property has been transferred to a child, grandchild, niece, or nephew, you must report any income earned on such property—such as interest or dividend income— until the child reaches 18 years of age. After 18, that individual must report the income. Capital gains, on the other hand, do not have to be attributed to you. This is a useful income-splitting tool.

TAX TIP

Unless the person receiving the property is your spouse or common-law partner, there is no requirement to attribute capital gains to you as the one who is doing the transfer. Consider buying capital property (such as equity-based mutual funds) with a low yield but high capital gains potential in the names of your children. The income will be attributed to you, but any future capital gains will be taxed in your children's hands.

Low-interest and interest-free loans

Caution should be exercised if you provide low-interest or interest-free loans to family members either to enable them to purchase income-producing assets or as consideration for the transfer of assets. If one of the main reasons for the loan is to reduce or avoid tax, you must report any income earned on the property regardless of the age of the person receiving the loan. An outright gift to a child, or anyone other than a spouse or common-law partner who is 18 or older, is not subject to this rule.

TAX TIP

Any involvement in transferring property or lending money to a spouse or common-law partner or other family members should have you consulting your tax adviser to ensure that the consequences of such transactions do not create a greater tax burden.

92 Registered education savings plans (RESPs)

An RESP is a type of trust through which you can save for a child's education. If the child does not pursue an education, the principal you contributed to the RESP is returned, but you may forfeit all of the earnings. Those earnings are then shared among other students in the plan who are pursuing a post-secondary education.

Contributions to such a plan are not tax-deductible, but the major advantage is that earnings accumulate on a tax-deferred basis. Also, when the funds are finally issued to the child, only the interest portion is considered income and is taxed at his or her lower rate.

Important changes

The annual contribution limit is $4,000 per beneficiary, subject to a lifetime limit of $42,000 per beneficiary. Several plans include a transferability feature that allows you to change the beneficiary or even to sell the plan should you conclude the designated child has no interest in post-secondary education.

To encourage the use of RESPs and minimize the risk of forfeited investment income, contributors may be able to receive RESP income directly in certain circumstances. If you made contributions to an RESP after 1997, and the plan has existed for at least 10 years but none of the intended beneficiaries are pursuing a higher education by the age of 21, you will be allowed to receive the RESP income and you may be allowed to transfer it to your RRSP (or your spouse or common-law partner's) if you have enough RRSP room to claim a deduction for the year of the transfer.

The total RESP income you can transfer to an RRSP is subject to a lifetime limit of $50,000. If the RESP income is not fully offset by RRSP deductions, the excess will be subject to a 20% penalty in addition to regular taxes.

More incentives introduced

A system of federal grants has been introduced to help the RESP earn income at a faster rate, a feature that makes these types of plans a somewhat more attractive vehicle to save for family members' post-secondary education.

Canada education savings grant (CESG)

Through the Canada education savings grant program, the government provides a sum equal to 20% of the first $2,000 of annual contributions to an RESP (up to $400 per year per child) for the benefit of children up to age 18. The grant is paid directly to the RESP and cannot exceed $7,200 for any one beneficiary.

For example, if you set up an RESP for your newborn son and make a $3,000 contribution during 2001, a CESG of $400 (i.e., 20% of $2,000) will be paid to the plan trustee. Together with the accumulating investment income and contributions, this amount will be available for educational assistance payments made out of the RESP.

When RESP funds are paid to a beneficiary, a formula will determine what portion of each payment is considered to be a distribution of the CESG. No single beneficiary may receive more than $7,200 of CESG from the plan.

If the contributor does not make a contribution to the RESP in one or more years, there are carry-forward provisions that can increase the CESG maximum from $400 to $800.

The grant is available for certain beneficiaries aged 17 and under in the year, and there are no restrictions for beneficiaries aged 15 and under in the year. In general, RESP contributions for children aged 16 and 17 in a particular year will be eligible for a grant only if contributions have been made for the child for at least four years, or if the previous contributions were at least $2,000. This means that a new plan will not get the CESG for a beneficiary who is 16 or 17. These age restrictions are in place to encourage early RESP savings.

An RESP will be required to repay CESG money in certain situations, such as if a beneficiary does not pursue higher education or if the plan is terminated.

93 Splitting CPP benefits with your spouse or common-law partner

The Canada Pension Plan Act permits you to assign a portion of your retirement pension to your spouse or common-law partner.

For example, suppose you are entitled to $6,000 in annual CPP benefits, but your spouse or common-law partner is entitled to only $1,200. This assignment will generally result in each of you receiving $3,600 annually. If your spouse or common-law partner is in a lower tax bracket than you, shifting this income to his or her hands helps lower the total family tax bill (see article **94**). The number of months you have both lived together is a factor in determining how the benefits are split.

If you both receive a CPP retirement pension, the assignment must be made for both retirement pensions. But if only one of you receives a retirement pension, the assignment can only be made if the other spouse or common-law partner has reached 60 years of age and is not a contributor to the CPP.

Divorced and separated couples

Although an assignment generally ceases on divorce, there are rules to permit you to apply for a share of the CPP credits of your former spouse if you were divorced after January 1, 1978. Also, CPP benefits can be split on the breakdown of a common-law relationship, provided you have lived together for at least one year and application is made within four years of the start of the separation. You can obtain application forms from your local Human Resources Development Canada office.

94 Income splitting with family members

Income splitting is a tax-planning technique designed to shift income from a taxpayer with a high rate to another taxpayer within the family unit with a lower rate. Unfortunately, there are a number of legislative provisions—"attribution rules"—designed to prevent saving taxes by shifting income between taxpayers (see article 91).

Permitted arrangements

Still, a number of legitimate tax-planning arrangements can be used to effectively redistribute income in a family unit. These include:

- having your business pay a reasonable salary to your spouse or common-law partner or children (see article 5)
- making contributions to a spousal RRSP (see articles 51–53)
- investing child tax benefit payments in your child's name (see article 83)
- sharing CPP payments with your spouse or common-law partner (see article 93)
- having the higher-income spouse or common-law partner assume most or all of the personal household expenses, leaving the person with the lower income with as much disposable income as possible to invest
- transferring or selling assets to family members at fair market value (see article 91)
- using a management company—although, if the management company provides services to a professional who provides tax-exempt services under the GST/HST, the taxable GST/HST charge will present an absolute increase in cost that may outweigh the income-splitting benefits of the management company
- creating testamentary trusts in your will to split income

- contributing to an RESP (see article **92**)
- giving cash or other assets to your adult children (see article **91**)
- having your spouse or common-law partner and/or adult children participate in an incorporated business by owning shares acquired with their own funds, which would allow company profits to be distributed to them in the form of dividends
- taking advantage of the fact that income earned on income is not subject to the attribution rules—although the initial income earned on property loaned to a non-arm's-length person may be attributed back to the person making the transfer, income earned on that income will not be attributed

EXAMPLE
Bypassing attribution

If you purchased $10,000 in 5% bonds on behalf of your 10-year-old son in 2000, he would receive $500 of interest on the bond in 2001. At that time, he invests the interest in additional 5% bonds. In 2002, your son will again receive interest of $500 on the original bonds, plus $25 on the bonds purchased in 2001. Although the $500 received by your son in both years is taxable in your hands, he reports the $25 received in 2001.

It's crucial that you confer with your tax adviser who can review your personal situation and give you advice regarding which income-splitting strategies best fit your circumstances.

95 Income splitting using family trusts
In the past, family trusts were used to provide a tax-effective way of splitting income with other family members. If properly structured, they could provide the following benefits:

- allow for flexibility in the payment of dividends to different family members
- provide multiple access to the qualified small business capital gains deduction

- provide some creditor-proofing for cash presently accumulated in your company
- minimize taxes paid by your family unit

Measures introduced a few years ago have eliminated many of the income-splitting benefits of family trusts and shareholdings by minors—but all is not lost. Many of the above benefits are still available, though possibly not to the same extent as in the past.

The new rules impose a "kiddie tax" on any child under 18 who receives taxable dividends from a private corporation, either directly or through a trust or other structure. The "kiddie tax" effectively charges the top marginal tax rate to the child on this type of income and therefore eliminates most of the tax savings that could be achieved by splitting income with minor children. These rules apply to certain dividends paid in 2000 and subsequent years—in general, taxable dividends received on shares of unlisted corporations. Income from property inherited from the minor's parent is excluded from this rule.

Where a trust has already been set up with minor children as the beneficiaries, and the trust holds shares in a private corporation, you still may be able to alter the structure, to retain some of its benefits. For example, where a trust holds the shares directly in a private operating company, a holding company can be placed between the operating company and the trust. The dividends from the operating company can then be paid into the holding company on a tax-free basis and held in the holding company until the beneficiaries of the trust are no longer minors.

Once the children turn 18—at which time dividends can begin to be paid out to them without the imposition of the "kiddie tax"—they can each receive approximately $25,000 per year in dividends without generating any tax liability (assuming they have no other income).

Based on your particular situation, other planning strategies may also be available.

TAX TIP

These new rules may affect many trusts, but, with proper planning, some of the benefits of these structures may be retained. Contact your tax adviser to review your situation and determine the best planning strategy.

96 Retroactive lump-sum payments

If you received a retroactive lump-sum payment in any year after 1994, you may be eligible to request a special tax calculation to provide tax relief. This calculation will effectively recompute your tax liability assuming the lump-sum payment had been taxed in the year(s) to which it relates. It will only be applied where the calculation results in a decreased tax liability.

The following types of income qualify for this calculation:

- periodic superannuation or pension benefits
- employment insurance benefits
- spousal or child support amounts
- employment income payments received under a court judgement or arbitration award

The lump-sum payment must be at least $3,000 and must have been received after 1994. The "qualifying amount" does not include any interest amount included in the payment.

TAX TIP

If you received a lump-sum retroactive payment in any year after 1994, contact your tax adviser to determine if you might benefit from requesting a recalculation of your tax return.

97 Some income is tax-free

Almost all types of income are subject to income tax—no surprise there. What *is* surprising is that a few exceptions are open to you.

If you are lucky enough to win a lottery in Canada, the amount you win is not taxable (but any income you receive from investing the money is taxable). Gains from casual gambling are not taxable. Proceeds from damage awards are generally tax-free and, under certain circumstances, income arising from damage awards for taxpayers under 21 years of age is also exempt until the taxpayer is 21. Various defined payments to war veterans are also exempt.

Workers' compensation benefits and welfare payments are also not directly subject to tax. However, they are a factor in determining eligibility for certain tax credits. The amounts must be included when computing net income. To arrive at taxable income, an offsetting deduction is permitted.

98 Taking up Canadian residence

Welcome to Canada.

For an individual who became a resident of Canada during 2001, there is a special set of income tax rules. For instance, all your capital property, except taxable Canadian property (see article **99**), will be deemed to have been acquired by you at its fair market value on the date you take up residence. Any gain or loss on a subsequent disposition of that property will be calculated on its value.

How much tax will you pay?

If you were not employed in Canada and had not carried on a business in Canada before becoming a resident, you are only taxed on your worldwide income from the date you become a resident of Canada. However, if you worked or carried on a business in Canada prior to becoming a resident, you will also be taxed on your income earned in Canada for that part of the year you were a non-resident.

You are entitled to claim personal tax credits, but the amounts are generally reduced on a pro rata basis according to the number of days in the year you are taxed on your worldwide income.

EXAMPLE

What you can claim

Suppose you are single, have no children, and immigrated to Canada on June 1, 2001. During the first part of the year, you were employed in a foreign country. You would be entitled to claim a basic personal amount of $4,346 ($7,412 × 214 ÷ 365).

If you arrived from a country that has a tax treaty with Canada, any provision in the treaty that conflicts with the Canadian tax rules will override the Canadian rule.

TAX TIP

Make sure that you are aware of the exemption from the new foreign reporting rules for the year in which you first become resident in Canada (see article **132**).

99 Giving up Canadian residence

Recent changes have altered the tax consequences to Canadians leaving Canada. In general, if you cease to be a resident of Canada, you will be deemed to have disposed of and reacquired all your capital property at its fair market value on that date and you will have to pay tax on any taxable capital gain resulting from this deemed disposition.

These deemed-disposition rules apply to all capital property other than Canadian real estate, Canadian business property, and certain other exclusions, such as retirement savings in RRSPs, stock options, and interest in some trusts. The most significant change is that unlisted shares, such as shares of a small private company, will now be subject to the deemed-disposition rules.

The implications

Tax triggered on the deemed disposition can either be paid when filing your income tax return or deferred until the property is actually sold. In that case, you must provide acceptable security to the CCRA. After you leave Canada, there may be further tax to pay. When you dispose of property excluded from the deemed-disposition rules, you are required to file a Canadian income tax return and pay tax on any resulting gain. In addition, when you actually dispose of capital property that has been subject to the deemed-disposition rules and that is considered "taxable Canadian property," you are required to file a Canadian income tax return. Additional Canadian tax may be payable on the gain accruing after you leave Canada.

Taxable Canadian property includes real property (such as land and buildings) located in Canada, capital property used in carrying on business in Canada, shares of a private corporation resident in Canada, and certain shares of public corporations.

Reporting requirement

If you emigrate from Canada, you are required to report your property holdings to the CCRA if you own property with a total value of more than $25,000 at the date of departure from Canada.

Exceptions will be provided for personal-use property with a value of less than $10,000. If you are subject to this reporting requirement, you should complete draft form T1161 and attach it to your income tax return for the year of departure.

TAX TIP

The capital gains deduction is not available to someone who is not a resident of Canada. If you have shares of a corporation that is a "qualified small business corporation" (see article 113), or have an interest in a farm operation (see article 114), there may be opportunities to utilize the $500,000 capital gains deduction. Review this with your tax adviser, as extensive planning is required.

Special rules apply if you leave Canada for only a few years to work or to study. The rules in this area are very complex. Therefore, if you are planning to leave Canada for any period of time, you should consult a tax specialist. In some cases, it may be beneficial to restructure your holdings prior to departure.

100 Temporary assignments outside Canada

Many assignments outside Canada are only temporary, ranging from a few weeks to several years. For income tax purposes, it is important that you determine your residency status during the period you are outside Canada. A resident of Canada is taxed on his or her worldwide income. Therefore, if you are a Canadian resident for income tax purposes, any income you earn during an assignment abroad will be subject to Canadian tax.

Residency defined

Residence is a question of fact and, surprisingly, the term "resident" is not defined in the Income Tax Act. The courts, however, have held that you are a resident of Canada for tax purposes if Canada is the place you regularly or customarily live.

The CCRA applies a general rule of thumb—unless the circumstances indicate otherwise, you will be considered a non-resident if you are absent from Canada for two years or longer. However, if your return to Canada is foreseeable at the time of departure, you will not necessarily lose your Canadian residency status for income tax purposes solely because of an absence of more than two years.

Canada also has income tax treaties with a number of countries, and these treaties contain tie-breaker rules to determine residency when you appear to be a resident of two countries.

TAX TIP

Depending on the circumstances, your residency status and the time of taking up residency may be difficult to ascertain. A discussion with your tax adviser is strongly recommended well in advance of any move into or out of Canada.

If you cease to be a resident of Canada for income tax purposes, special rules apply (see article **99**).

101 U.S. citizens resident in Canada

The United States taxes its citizens on their worldwide income whether they live in the United States or not. As a result, if you are a U.S. citizen living in Canada, you are required to file a tax return under both systems.

Watch out for tax liabilities

Although there are several mechanisms in place to prevent double taxation, there are still many differences between the two tax systems that can lead to unexpected tax liabilities. One of the most glaring is in the area of capital gains. For this reason, you should always obtain professional tax advice if you have sold or are considering selling capital property.

TAX TIP

If your income is high enough, you may also have to pay a certain amount of U.S. alternative minimum tax even though your income is fully taxed in Canada. Be aware of this potential liability when planning your income.

Filing your returns

For Canadian tax purposes, each taxpayer must file a separate return. For U.S. tax purposes, you have the option of filing a joint return with your spouse. If your spouse has little or no income but you are paying tax to the United States, filing a joint election will generally be beneficial.

If your spouse is not a U.S. citizen, you can still file a joint return, but the rules are a little more complicated. First, you must file an election to treat your non-resident spouse as a U.S. citizen. Once this election is made, your spouse must file a U.S. income tax return each year until the election is revoked. Once revoked, the election cannot be reinstated. During the years in which the election is in force, you and your spouse may decide annually whether to elect to file a joint return. This decision can change from year to year. A discussion with your tax adviser is recommended.

If you are a U.S. citizen, you may be required to file a return even if no U.S. tax is owing. Several years ago, the Internal Revenue Service (IRS) launched a "non-filer program" in an attempt to bring back into the U.S. tax system taxpayers who have not been filing returns. Substantial resources are being devoted to finding non-filers who are likely to owe a significant amount.

An IRS information return must now be completed in conjunction with the processing of all passport applications. If you have not been filing a U.S. return, you should get professional advice. As well as filing a tax return, you may also be required to disclose a substantial amount of other financial information to the U.S. government.

102 U.S. social security payments

Over the past few years, the taxation of social security payments from the United States has been subject to a good deal of change and confusion.

Current rules

Under the most recent rules, U.S. social security benefits received by residents of Canada are only subject to tax in Canada. The United States will not tax these benefits.

The full amount of the benefit received will be included in net income, but 15% of that amount will be deductible in computing taxable income. As a result, only 85% of the benefits received in a year will be subject to tax. But the full amount is included in net income for assessing various clawbacks and other net income-based calculations—the OAS clawback (see article **66**) and the age credit (see article **82**).

103 U.S. real estate owned by Canadian residents

For Canadian residents who receive rent from U.S. real estate, a withholding tax of 30% normally applies to the gross amount of any rent paid. As an alternative, you can elect to pay tax on a net income basis. In this case, you must file a U.S. tax return at the end of the year, reporting your net rental income. By making this election with the IRS and providing appropriate information to the tenant, the 30% withholding tax is not required. Once you make this election, it is permanent and can only be revoked in limited circumstances.

Many people assume that because their expenses always exceed their rental income, there is no need to file a U.S. tax return or to have tax withheld at source. However, if tax is not withheld at source, a tax return must be filed within a certain time period if you want to claim expenses.

TAX TIP

Professional advice is the best remedy if you receive rental income from U.S. real property and have not filed a U.S. return because your expenses exceed your rental income. The U.S. has strict rules regarding the timely filing of such returns. If the returns are not filed by a specified deadline, you will not be entitled to claim any deductions and tax will be assessed on the gross income.

Selling your U.S. property

Selling your U.S. real property? Then expect to pay a 10% withholding tax. However, this withholding will not apply if the property is sold for less than US$300,000 and the purchaser intends to use the property as a residence. Also, you can apply to the IRS to have the withholding tax reduced if the expected tax liability on the sale will be less than 10% of the sale price.

Regardless of the amount of withholding tax, the gain on the sale of any U.S. property is still taxable in the United States and a U.S. tax return must be filed. The U.S. tax that applies generates a foreign tax credit that can be used to reduce the Canadian tax on the sale. If you have owned the property continuously since before September 27, 1980, for personal use only, a provision of the Canada-U.S. tax treaty can be used to reduce the gain.

104 U.S. estate tax

The estate of a deceased Canadian could be subject to U.S. estate tax on the full value of the deceased's taxable estate located in the United States. Tax is applied on the value of the U.S. property. The major types of assets subject to U.S. estate tax are U.S. real property, shares of U.S. companies, tangible personal property located in the U.S., and debts issued by U.S. residents, including the U.S. government.

However, there is good news—the Canada-U.S. tax treaty may provide significant relief in this area. First, regardless of your U.S. holdings, you are not subject to U.S. estate tax if the value of your worldwide gross estate is less than US$675,000. This exemption will continue to increase gradually to $3.5 million by the year 2009 and it is proposed that the estate tax will be completely repealed in 2010. For non-U.S. citizens, the exemption must be pro-rated, based on the percentage of a Canadian resident's worldwide wealth that is covered by the estate tax net. A Canadian resident having a worldwide estate with a value in US$'s that is less than the exemption will not be subject to any estate tax. Obviously, the higher a non-U.S. citizen's worldwide wealth in relation to his or her U.S. holdings, the greater his or her exposure to estate tax. If any Canadian tax is payable—due to the deemed disposition on death rules—a foreign tax credit can be claimed for any U.S. estate taxes that have to be paid (to a maximum of the Canadian tax payable).

TAX TIP

Do you own or are you about to acquire property situated in the United States? If so, consult your tax adviser to review your exposure to U.S. federal estate tax. Planning strategies are available to defer, reduce, or eliminate this potential liability.

TAX TIP

If you are the beneficiary of the estate of a U.S. resident, seek professional tax advice. Without planning, cross-border estates often experience double tax, since the tax systems of Canada and the U.S. are not necessarily coordinated.

105 U.S. residency regulations

Many Canadians who regularly spend winters in the United States may find that they are required to fill out a special declaration—the "Closer Connection Exemption Statement"—to be exempt from American taxes.

Are you exempt?

To determine whether you are one of the Canadians who should file this declaration, you must add up the number of days (or part-days) you spent in the United States in 2001, one-third of the days in 2000, and one-sixth of the days in 1999. If this calculation adds up to 183 days or more, you may be considered a U.S. resident for tax purposes.

However, you can qualify for the "closer connection" exemption if you meet certain provisions. These include that you have not applied for a U.S. green card, were present in the United States for less than 183 days in 2001, have maintained a permanent place of residence in Canada throughout 2001, can claim a closer connection to Canada, and file the special declaration by June 15, 2002.

Green-card holders are not entitled to file this declaration. If you hold a green card, or if you spent more than 182 days in the United States in the current year, you will have to rely on the tie-breaker rules in the Canada-U.S. treaty to avoid U.S. resident status. As a cautionary note, U.S. Immigration has issued a warning to green-card holders that they may jeopardize their green-card status if they use treaty provisions to be taxed as a non-resident of the United States.

TAX TIP

Over the past several years, the United States has issued numerous rules and regulations of concern to Canadians with interests in that country. If you spend a considerable amount of time in the U.S. each year, contact your tax adviser to ensure you are complying with these rules.

106 Withholding tax for non-resident actors

If you pay amounts to a non-resident who provides film or video acting services in Canada, new rules impose a 23% withholding tax on the gross amount paid to the non-resident person (either to the individual or a corporation related to the individual). These rules only apply to acting income—they do not apply to other services performed within the movie industry, such as those provided by directors, producers, and other personnel working behind the scenes. Also, these rules do not apply to persons in other sectors of the entertainment industry, such as musical performers, ice or air show performers, or international speakers. There are special rules where the recipient of the payment is a corporation that employs the actor.

Non-resident actors have the option of filing a tax return to recover some of the amount withheld. However, whether the recipient chooses this option or not, you are still required to withhold and remit to the Receiver General 23% of any amounts paid.

This new system applies to acting services payments made after 2000.

The following transitional provisions will be in place for the 2001 taxation year:

- Non-resident actors who entered into agreements before January 1, 2001, will be subject to the 15% withholding rate on services they provide in Canada throughout the 2001 calendar year.
- The payer will be required to obtain written certification that the agreement was entered into before January 1, 2001. This certification must be signed by the actor (or his or her representative).
- Non-resident actors who entered into agreements after December 31, 2000, will be subject to the flat 23% withholding rate.
- All services provided after 2001 will be subject to the 23% withholding—regardless of when the agreement was entered into.

107 Estate planning

Estate planning is a difficult subject to deal with briefly. It is simply not possible to advise people on such matters without considerable reference to other areas of taxation and to personal and financial objectives.

Estate planning means different things to different people, and it is an ongoing process. However, it primarily means arranging your financial affairs during your lifetime in such a way that income taxes and estate administration fees are minimized upon death and the estate will have sufficient liquidity to pay income taxes and other liabilities arising on death.

Estate planning can include such things as:

- transferring assets to family members during one's lifetime
- capping the value of growth assets at their current values by transferring future asset appreciation to other family members (estate freezing)
- probate planning
- planned giving
- preparation of a will
- acquisition of life insurance if needed to fund an income tax liability

Asset transfers

If you have decided that you have more assets than you need, you can reduce your estate probate fees and executor fees, and possibly income taxes upon death, if you transfer assets to your children or other family members during your lifetime. However, if these assets have increased in value since acquisition, the transfer could cause an income tax liability. Carefully assess which assets to transfer and how to avoid triggering a tax hit.

TAX TIP

For those fortunate enough to have assets that can provide an income larger than lifetime needs, gifting some of the assets to beneficiaries during your lifetime is a logical way to reduce taxes. Complicated rules exist regarding income and capital gains on gifts to spouses or common-law partners and children under 18 (see article **91**).

Freezing your estate

Estate freezing is a popular method of limiting death taxes. It primarily consists of transferring the growth potential of assets such as real estate or shares of corporations to a younger generation. By doing so, the value of the asset to the person doing the transfer is frozen at its value at the date of transfer. Accordingly, the amount of potential capital gain on death is also frozen. One can better plan for the payment of income taxes on death if one can reasonably estimate the amount of potential taxes, as would be the case if the capital gain is frozen.

You can usually accomplish an estate freeze through a transfer of assets to a corporation or an internal reorganization of capital. The mechanics can vary, but the transfer must be professionally planned in order to avoid running afoul of the many punitive provisions of the Income Tax Act.

Alter-ego and joint-partner trusts

In order to avoid probate fees, substitutes for wills—such as inter vivos trusts—have been used to transfer assets to the next generation. However, a gift of assets to a non-spousal trust that names other persons as beneficiaries usually results in a disposition of those assets at fair market value for income tax purposes. This can result in the payment of significant tax at the time of the transfer.

If you are 65 years of age or over, recent legislative changes will make it easier for you to take advantage of such trusts. These new rules, which apply to trusts established after 1999, introduce the concepts of alter-ego and joint-partner trusts. One of the advantages of these types of trusts is that assets can be transferred to them on a tax-deferred basis, thereby avoiding triggering tax on accrued gains. However, there will be a deemed disposition of all property in the trust on the later of the day you or (where applicable) your spouse or partner dies. Another advantage is that they can avoid the application of wills variation legislation (in those provinces that have this legislation).

The main disadvantage is that the assets in the trust cannot be transferred to a continuing testamentary trust after death, thereby providing for graduated tax rates after death.

If you establish an alter-ego or joint-partner trust, you (or you in combination with your spouse or common-law partner) must be entitled to receive all of the income of the trust prior to death. Also, no person can obtain the use of any income or capital of the trust before your death (or that of your surviving spouse or common-law partner in the case of a joint-partner trust).

TAX TIP

If you own assets with an accrued gain, talk to your financial adviser about the advisability of setting up an alter-ego or joint-partner trust.

Planned giving

The value of your estate can be reduced by making charitable donations during your lifetime (see article **75**). The added benefit is that you also earn income tax credits during your life rather than for your estate. Over the past few years, several rules have been introduced to encourage the private funding of charitable organizations. For example:

- the general annual limit on charitable donations as a percentage of net income has risen from 20% to 75%;
- the limit on gifts by individuals in the year of death and prior year has risen to 100% of net income; and
- there are reduced capital gains inclusion rates where certain types of appreciated capital property are donated to a registered charity—for example, donations of publicly listed securities (see article **75**).

Through effective plans for giving, you can balance your personal financial goals and your charitable interests while realizing significant tax benefits. Other benefits can include reducing probate fees and other estate costs.

Some of the planned-giving opportunities available are as follows.

Gifts of life insurance

Life insurance can be used to provide a relatively large endowment to a registered charity on your death while requiring comparatively modest cash outflows during your lifetime. The gift can be in the form of a new or an existing whole life insurance policy. Where an existing policy is donated, the donation receipt will be for the value of the policy, which is generally measured as the cash surrender value of the policy plus any accumulated dividends and interest. The continuing payment of insurance premiums on behalf of the charity will also result in a donation receipt. However, for the charity to acquire an interest in the policy, there must be an absolute and unconditional assignment of all rights, title, and interest in the policy.

Charitable annuities

Some charities have the legal right to issue annuities. In this case, you make a contribution of capital to the charity. In return, the charity agrees to make periodic payments to you for either a specified period or for life. If you pay more for the annuity than the total amount you are expected to receive from the registered charity, the excess amount is considered a gift to the charity. In general, the annuity payments are not taxable. Those charities that cannot issue annuities themselves acquire the annuity from a third party.

Charitable remainder trusts

The most common form of a charitable remainder trust is an irrevocable trust that holds property that you want to contribute to a specified charity. The real attractiveness of this type of vehicle is the ability to make the gift on an inter vivos basis while guaranteeing you the right to enjoy the use of the property or the revenue from investments during your lifetime. You receive an immediate tax receipt for the present value of the remainder interest in the property. For example, you might consider donating the remainder interest in your personal residence. No tax results on the disposition of a personal residence (see article **89**), and the donation receipt can be used to shelter tax on other sources of income while you are still alive.

The main disadvantage of these trusts is that once the donation is made, you cannot change your mind and take the property back.

Use of private foundations

Private foundations have the advantage of providing you with an immediate donation receipt for the amount contributed to the foundation while at the same time allowing you to retain control of the funds and delay the distribution of capital to qualifying charities (subject to special rules).

Planned giving does not have to be as complex as the above strategies might imply. It may simply involve reviewing your charitable objectives with a view to accelerating your intended donations now to maximize tax savings.

Since many of the planned-giving strategies involve the disposition of capital, you may also have to report income or a capital gain as a result of making the gift. As the name suggests, planned giving consists of planning and giving. Planning refers to a careful consideration of estate planning, financial planning, and tax planning as part of making the gift. Your tax adviser can assist in helping you develop a planned-giving strategy that is most appropriate to your individual situation.

TAX TIP

Planning to make significant charitable donations through your estate? It may not be your best option. If you make them during your lifetime, you will reduce the value of your estate for probate purposes, reduce your executor fees, and get tax savings earlier.

Preparing a will

On death, you are deemed to have disposed of all capital property at fair market value, with the exception of property passing to a spouse or common-law partner or to certain trusts created for the benefit of a spouse or common-law partner. This deemed disposition can create a very large income tax bill.

Both you and your spouse or common-law partner should have wills. This is probably one of the most critical elements of your estate-planning strategy, as dying intestate (without a will) can defeat almost all the arrangements you have put into place.

TAX TIP

A periodic review of your will is part of prudent estate planning. It should be done to ensure that your assets will be dealt with in the most tax-effective manner and that your will complies with current laws, such as provincial family law acts.

Life insurance

Sometimes, just as you can't avoid death, it is also not possible to avoid taxes when you die. If your estate has enough liquid assets, paying income taxes may not be much of a problem. But, if a major portion of your estate consists of shares of private companies or real estate, it may not be possible to satisfy your tax bill on death, at least not without sell-ing off the assets.

Funding potential income taxes through the purchase of life insurance is often a most effective estate-planning tool. If sufficient insurance pro-ceeds are available, any income tax arising on the deemed dispositions of assets on your death can be paid without resorting to the sale of your assets. And having to sell off the assets means, of course, they cannot be passed on to beneficiaries.

In recent years, the investment aspect of some life insurance policies has become more attractive. One of the major reasons for this is the favourable tax treatment provided for "exempt" policies. Any investment income earned in such a policy is exempt from tax. In addition, any amounts paid out under such a policy on the death of the insured are also exempt from tax. This tax shelter aspect of an exempt policy has several potential uses, particularly after other tax shelter opportunities such as RRSPs have been exhausted. For example, such a policy could be used in connection with a shareholder buy-sell agreement. You may also be able to get at the tax-sheltered earnings through taxable draws on the cash sur-render value of the policy, or by pledging the policy as collateral for a loan.

To be exempt, a policy must satisfy certain complex rules. Also, as with any other tax shelter, an investment in an exempt policy should be assessed on its merits.

TAX TIP

You have made the decision to acquire life insurance to fund any income taxes that may arise from the deemed disposition of shares of a private corporation. Plan carefully to determine whether you, rather than your company, should own the policy. Both options have different advantages. A consultation with your tax and insurance advisers is a must.

Investors

Being an investor means earning money. And whenever money is earned, the tax collector is never far behind. This section includes over two dozen items that outline what you can do and can't do for tax relief as you put your money to work.

In this section, we discuss rental properties, capital gains and the capital gains deduction, business investment losses, and capital loss rules. We also look at such investment vehicles as Canada savings bonds and mutual funds, examine issues associated with demutualizations, and fully explain the taxation of interest and dividend income, and the deductibility of interest expenses.

We also address the use of the resource sector as a tax shelter, and limited partnerships. If you have earned investment income from foreign sources, you can find out your tax obligations in that respect while also learning more about the new foreign reporting requirements. To round out the section, we've provided numerous tax tips that illuminate some of the strategies you can and should use to your advantage as you build your portfolio.

108 Rental properties

If you owned a rental property in 2001, any net income or loss must be reported on your 2001 income tax return. Rental income is usually reported on a calendar-year basis because the earnings are classified as property income and not as business income. Any income or loss from a rental property you own outside of Canada must also be included in your return.

What can I deduct?

All reasonable expenses incurred in operating the property can be deducted. This can include the cost of insurance, property taxes, mortgage interest, power supply, heat, repairs, and even advertising for tenants. If you borrowed money to make the down payment, interest on that loan is also deductible. In certain circumstances, you may also be able to claim depreciation.

TAX TIP

Keep accurate records of all expenses relating to your rental property. Retain all receipts and make a small note on each one pointing out what the money was spent on and why. This will help your adviser quickly determine if it's a valid expense and eligible for deduction or depreciation.

What can I depreciate?

In general, depreciation on a rental property cannot be used to either create or increase your rental loss. When more than one rental property is owned, all of the net rental income (or loss) is combined to determine the total income or loss for the year.

Depreciation may only be claimed on the property to the extent of any net income from the rental of these properties before depreciation. Net income for determining the amount of depreciation you can claim includes recaptured depreciation on another rental property.

TAX TIP

If capital costs are required, try to time them for the end of the year instead of the first of the following year. This will speed up your tax depreciation expense. In other words, you will be able to start depreciating it immediately instead of having to wait another 12 months.

What happens if I sell?

Two different types of income may arise on the sale of your rental property. If you sell your property for more than its original cost, you have to report a capital gain. If the property was purchased before February, 1992, some or all of this gain may have been eligible for the capital gains deduction. To take advantage of this, however, you should have made a special election on filing your 1994 return (see article **112**).

What else should I be aware of?

You may also have to pay tax on income that represents previously claimed depreciation. If proceeds from the sale exceed the undepreciated capital cost (UCC) of the property, the excess, up to the original cost, is taxed as recaptured depreciation in the year of sale.

If the proceeds are more than the original cost, there will be a full recapture and a capital gain. And if the proceeds are less than the original cost but greater than the UCC, there will be no capital gain and the recapture will be measured as the difference between the proceeds and the UCC. In some cases, where the property was destroyed or expropriated and another property was purchased, the gain and/or recapture may be deferred.

EXAMPLE

The UCC factor

You purchased a building in 1992 at a cost of $100,000 and the UCC at the end of 2000 was $80,000. If you sell the building in 2001 for $120,000, you will have to report recapture of $20,000 and a capital gain of $20,000. If you sell the building for $90,000, you will have to report recapture of $10,000 and there is no capital gain to report.

Anything else?

You may have a terminal loss if the proceeds of the sale are less than the UCC of the property, and this loss is deductible from your other sources of income. In the past, the tax department often disallowed such losses on the basis that the taxpayer had "no reasonable expectation of profit." However, in a 1996 court case, the presiding judge found that this test should be used sparingly where it is evident that a loss does not have a personal or non-business motive. The same applies in determining whether rental losses should be deductible.

Also, if you did not receive the full proceeds of the sale in the year of the sale, you may be able to claim a capital gains reserve (see article **116**). However, you cannot claim any reserve against the recaptured depreciation.

109 Terminal loss restrictions

When you sell a building at a loss, certain rules may reduce the loss for tax purposes. If the building was sold together with the underlying land, the transaction is treated as if you sold two separate items. If the portion of the sale price attributed to the building is less than its undepreciated cost, you may be required to increase the portion allocated to the building and reduce the portion allocated to the land. This will result in a reduced terminal loss on the building.

These rules only apply to depreciable buildings and do not apply to a real estate developer who is holding real estate as inventory.

⬛110 Joint owner or partner?

If you acquired a partial interest in a rental property, it is important to know whether it is in a partnership or in a joint venture. If you do not know which it is, consult your tax adviser.

With an interest in a partnership, you must report your share of its net profit or loss on your personal tax return. Depreciation is computed at the partnership level, not by each individual partner.

As a joint owner, you have to report your share of the revenue and expenses related to the property. Next, you compute depreciation based upon the cost of your share of the property. Your depreciation claim is independent of the depreciation that may be claimed by the other joint owners.

TAX TIP

Where rental properties are owned in a partnership and outside a partnership, a reorganization of ownership may allow increased depreciation charges. Consult your tax adviser on the merits of restructuring.

GST/HST reporting

Reporting requirements under the GST/HST also differ depending on ownership status. If the property is held as a partnership, the partnership determines whether it is required to register. If the partnership registers, GST/HST returns are filed by the partnership, not the individual partners. If the property is held as a joint venture, the individual members are required to register and file GST/HST returns. In certain cases, an election is available to allow one member of the joint venture to file on behalf of any or all of the members.

▓ What about capital gains?

A capital gain occurs when you sell a capital property for more than its original cost. In general, where the disposition takes place after October 17, 2000, one-half of the gain is added to your other income for the year. The other one-half of the gain is not subject to tax. For dispositions before February 28, 2000, the capital gains inclusion rate was three-quarters, while the rate was reduced to two-thirds for dispositions between February 28 and October 17, 2000.

When is a gain a capital gain?

Due to the lower inclusion rate, it is beneficial to have a disposition taxed as a capital gain. In most circumstances, there is no set rule that determines whether a particular gain should be treated as a capital gain. Most individuals who invest in the stock market can treat their gains and losses as capital gains or losses. However, if you spend considerable time playing the market and/or borrow money to make your purchases, your profits or losses may be taxed in full as business income.

Similarly, if you bought a property intentionally to resell at a profit, the entire gain would be taxable (rather than just one-half). For example, taxpayers who purchase property for immediate resale, called "flipping," are subject to tax on the full gain even though they may have spent little time on the venture and may have sold only one or two properties. In some cases, there is no clear-cut answer. If in doubt, consult your tax adviser.

TAX TIP

Most taxpayers can elect capital gains treatment from the disposition of qualifying Canadian securities by filing form T123. However, once you make the election, all subsequent gains and losses from the disposition of qualifying securities will be recorded as capital gains and losses. Be sure you understand the implications of making this election before you file the form.

Capital gains from a partnership

Any income allocated from a partnership to a partner is included in the partner's income for the year in which the fiscal year of the partnership ends. For example, if a partnership with a June 30, 2001, year-end realized a capital gain on November 1, 2000, a partner who is an individual will report the gain on his or her tax return for the year 2001.

Capital gains (or losses) reported in 2000 were subject to three different inclusion rates, depending on when the gain (or loss) was realized (see p. 149, top). However, the rules with respect to partnerships provided that a capital gain (or loss) from a partnership was to be adjusted to reflect the partner's overall inclusion rate for the year. Therefore, capital gains and losses allocated from a partnership in the year 2000 could have been subject to an inclusion rate anywhere between 50% and 75%, depending on the other gains and losses reported for the year. In some cases, the information slips prepared for the CCRA (form T5013) incorrectly reported the allocation of capital gains and losses from a partnership. If you reported a capital gain or loss from a partnership for the year 2000, you should contact your tax adviser to see if any adjustments are required.

Identical properties

Subject to the special rules for stock option shares (see opposite), when you acquire securities that are exactly the same—for example, class A common shares of XYZ Corp.—the shares are pooled to determine your cost when you sell a portion of the shares.

EXAMPLE

Assume you buy 100 shares today for $20 each (total cost $2,000) and 50 shares next month for $26 each (total cost $1,300). Your cost per share for tax purposes is $22 (150 shares for a total cost of $3,300). If you then sell 75 shares for $30 each, your capital gain is $600 [($30 − $22) × 75 shares].

Special rules apply if you own identical properties, some of which were acquired before 1972. In this case, two separate pools will determine the cost of the properties sold, one comprising the pre-1972 properties and the other for properties acquired after 1971. On a disposition, you will be deemed to have sold the pre-1972 properties before those acquired after 1971.

Sale of stock option shares

The cost base of shares acquired through stock option plans equals the sum of the option price plus the amount of the taxable employment benefit. The amount of a deferred stock option benefit (see article **34**) is added to the cost base of the stock option share at the time the share is acquired, even though the amount is not taxed until the share is disposed of.

But what happens if you acquire shares under a company stock option plan and you already own other identical shares in the company, or if you exercise more than one stock option at the same time? If you sell only some of the shares, how do you calculate the tax cost of the shares sold? The rules in this area are extremely complex. There are special rules that deem the order in which the shares are disposed of. In addition, in certain cases, a special designation may be available that permits you to designate the new stock option shares as the shares being sold, provided they are sold within 30 days of exercising the option.

TAX TIP

Before selling or otherwise disposing of shares acquired under a stock option plan, consult your tax adviser to determine the tax consequences and whether you qualify for the special designation.

112 Lifetime capital gains deduction

In 1985, every Canadian became eligible for a limited lifetime capital gains deduction. However, in 1994, it was eliminated for dispositions of property after February 22, 1994, other than shares of qualified small business corporations (see article **113**) and qualified farm property (see article **114**).

$100,000 capital gains deduction

Other property having an accrued gain on February 22, 1994, was eligible for the $100,000 capital gains deduction if you made a special one-time-only "capital gains election." In most cases, this election had to be made on your 1994 tax return, and it allowed you to opt to have a deemed disposition of any capital property you owned on February 22, 1994, at any amount up to its fair market value on that day.

Depending on the type of capital property, the amount you elected as a deemed disposition became your new cost base. Or, in some cases, the gain created a special tax account that could be used to reduce a gain on that property in later years (see articles **8** and **123**). The election was made by filing form T664 with your income tax return.

TAX TIP

If you still own property for which a capital gains election was made, you should continue to monitor the revised cost base to ensure it is taken into consideration upon a subsequent sale of the property.

113 Qualified small business corporations capital gains deduction

Shares of a qualified small business corporation (QSBC) continue to qualify for an enhanced $500,000 capital gain deduction. To be eligible as a QSBC, a company must be a Canadian-controlled private corporation, at least 90% of its assets must be used in an active business in Canada, and additional conditions must be met for up to two years before the sale. Further complications may arise where there are investments in other related companies.

Each individual is entitled to a cumulative capital gains deduction of $500,000. As a result, the $500,000 capital gain deduction available on the disposition of QSBC shares will be reduced by the amount of the capital gains deductions previously claimed on any property.

EXAMPLE

Capital gains deduction at work

Let's assume you elected on your 1994 tax return to have a deemed disposition (see article **112**) of shares of public companies, and you claimed a capital gains deduction of $100,000. In 2001, you realize a $500,000 capital gain on the sale of shares of a qualified small business corporation. You are only entitled to a $400,000 capital gains deduction in 2001 because you used $100,000 of your $500,000 lifetime capital gains deduction in 1994. However, if you had previously only claimed a $60,000 capital gains deduction, you would be entitled to a $440,000 capital gains deduction in 2001.

The amount of capital gain that is eligible for the capital gains deduction may be affected by the balance in your cumulative net investment loss (CNIL) account (see article **126**) and whether or not you have ever claimed an allowable business investment loss (ABIL) (see article **118**).

TAX TIP

To qualify as a QSBC at the time of sale, it may be necessary to take steps now to remove non-qualifying assets from the company.

Although the $500,000 deduction continues to be available, it may be appropriate to consider various tax-planning techniques that can be used to obtain the deduction. The end result of most of these planning strategies will be to increase the cost base of your shares for purposes of a future sale or deemed disposition. Professional tax advice on these matters is a must.

Election for private companies going public

Shares of a public corporation do not qualify for the enhanced capital gains deduction. However, if you own shares in a small business corporation that is about to go public, you can make an election to be treated as having disposed of all of the shares of a class of the capital stock of the small business corporation immediately before it becomes a public corporation. You can elect an amount as the deemed proceeds of disposition that can be anywhere between the cost and fair market value of the shares. The shares are deemed to be reacquired for that same amount. In this way, you can benefit from claiming the enhanced capital gains deduction in respect of the shares.

ⅢⅢ Qualified farm property capital gains deduction

Qualified farm property is also eligible for a $500,000 capital gain deduction that will be reduced by the amount of capital gains deductions claimed on other property. And again, the amount eligible for this deduction may be affected by the balance in your CNIL account (see article **126**) and whether or not you have ever claimed an ABIL (see article **118**).

What qualifies?

In general, if you acquired certain property before June 18, 1987, and it was used in the business of farming by you or a member of your family, it will be qualified farm property, provided the property was used for farming in the year you sell it or in any five previous years during which you or a member of your family owned it.

If you acquired the property after June 17, 1987, you must normally have owned it for at least two years, been engaged in farming on a regular and continuous basis, and earned more gross income from farming than from other sources. Similar rules also apply to allow the deduction to be claimed for gains realized on the sale of shares of a family farm corporation and on an interest in a family farm partnership.

However, if you made a capital gains election (see article 112) on property that would otherwise be considered qualified farm property, the qualifying tests may be different from those outlined above. Discuss this with your tax adviser.

TAX TIP

Professional advice from your tax adviser is recommended to determine if you are eligible for the $500,000 deduction on your farm property (or property that was formerly used in farming).

115 Capital gains deferral for investment in small businesses

To increase the availability of equity capital for small business corporations, individuals can defer tax on up to $2 million of capital gains if the proceeds from the disposition of a qualified small business investment are reinvested in another eligible small business investment. Newly issued common shares in a small business corporation with assets not exceeding $50 million after the investment are the eligible investments, and these new rules apply to capital gains realized after October 17, 2000. For capital gains realized after February 27 and before October 18, 2000, the capital gain that could be deferred was only $500,000 and the size of new investments was limited to businesses with assets not exceeding $2.5 million before and $10 million after the investment.

To qualify, the proceeds must be reinvested in other eligible small business investments by the earlier of 120 days after the disposition or 60 days after the end of the year. The cost base of the new investment is reduced by the capital gain deferred.

EXAMPLE

On April 30, 2001, you sell shares of an eligible small business investment for $200,000 and realize a capital gain of $160,000. On July 1, 2001, you invest $180,000 of the proceeds to acquire shares of an eligible business investment. The capital gain that can be deferred is $144,000 [($180,000 ÷ $200,000) × $160,000].

Capital gain for 2001	$160,000
Less deferred gain	(144,000)
Net gain for 2001	$ 16,000

Cost of new investment:	
Amount invested	$180,000
Less deferred gain	(144,000)
Revised cost base	$ 36,000

If you sell this new investment for $220,000 in 2004, you will realize a capital gain of $184,000 at that time ($220,000 − $36,000).

116 Capital gains reserves may be restricted

When you sell your real estate or another investment, and the proceeds from the sale will not all be receivable in the year of sale, you can defer a portion of the capital gain by claiming a reserve.

The rules provide that at least one-fifth of your taxable capital gain must be reported in the year of sale and each of the four following years. An exception is provided if you transfer certain farm property or shares in a small business corporation to your children. In these cases, you can claim a reserve over a maximum 10-year period. Reserves deducted from income in one year must be added to income in the subsequent year.

TAX TIP

Claiming a reserve is optional—any amount up to the maximum allowed can be claimed. To make a claim, you must file form T2017 with your income tax return.

Special rules

Capital gains reserves included in income will be eligible for the capital gains deduction if the property was disposed of after 1984 and is a share of a qualified small business corporation or a qualified farm property (see articles **113** and **114**). Special rules are provided to ensure that reserves are adjusted for changes in the capital gains inclusion rate.

Should you decide to report all of the capital gain and claim the off-setting capital gains deduction, even though a reserve is available, take care to ensure you are not caught by the alternative minimum tax (see article **133**) or the cumulative net investment loss rules (see article **126**).

TAX TIP

In structuring the sale of property, make sure you will have enough funds to pay the taxes required. If proceeds are deferred over a long period of time, the tax may be due before the proceeds are received. Suppose you sell real estate for a significant capital gain in 2001 and the proceeds are due over the next six years. The taxes arising on the capital gain must be paid in full by 2005 even though some of the proceeds are not due until 2006.

117 Capital loss rules

Generally, capital losses are only deductible against capital gains. But there are cases where unused allowable capital losses realized prior to May 23, 1985, can be claimed against other sources of income at the rate of $2,000 per year. After that date, capital losses can only be claimed against capital gains. Capital losses can be carried back three years and forward indefinitely.

Restrictions on claims

The introduction of the capital gains deduction in 1985 was accompanied by rules to ensure you would not be able to claim the deduction and deduct capital losses from other sources at the same time. If you claimed pre-May 23, 1985, losses against other sources of income, and realized a capital gain on the disposition of shares of a qualified small business corporation or a qualified farm property, the amount of the gain eligible for the capital gains deduction could be affected.

There are also special rules that will deny a capital loss in certain situations. For example, if you transfer a property with an accrued loss to an "affiliated person," the loss will be denied. In general, you are affiliated with yourself and your spouse or common-law partner and with a corporation that you and/or your spouse or common-law partner control—but not with your children.

TAX TIP

This is a complex area and care must be taken to ensure you do not end up with unintended results. In particular, if you are acquiring or disposing of capital property and corporations, trusts, or partnerships in which you have an interest or are involved, professional advice is a must.

Similar rules will deny the loss if you sell investments with an accrued loss, and the same or identical property is acquired by you or your spouse or common-law partner within the period beginning 30 days before and ending 30 days after the disposition, and it is still owned 30 days after the disposition.

Rules are also in effect to adjust prior years' capital loss carryforwards for changes in the capital gains inclusion rate.

Unused capital losses from prior years may be claimed in the year of death or the immediately preceding year, first to reduce capital gains in those years. Any remaining capital losses may then be deducted from other sources of income, subject to a restriction based on the total capital gains deduction that has been claimed over the years. As these special rules on the deductibility of capital losses for deceased persons are quite complex, consult your tax adviser for further details.

TAX TIP

If you realized a capital gain in the current year, consider selling investments with accrued losses before the end of the year. Keep in mind that transactions involving publicly traded securities take place on the settlement date that is generally three days after the trading date in the case of Canadian stock exchanges.

TAX TIP

Don't sell your losers to your RRSP. Losses arising on the sale of capital property to an RRSP will be denied. You would be better off selling the investment to an unrelated party and making a cash contribution to your plan.

118 Business investment losses

By realizing a capital loss on the disposition of shares or debt of a small business corporation, you may be eligible to treat the loss as a business investment loss. One-half of this loss can be applied against your income from other sources, not just capital gains. If the disposition took place before October 18, 2000, the portion of the loss that could be deducted from your other income was either three-quarters or two-thirds, depending on when the property was sold (see article 111).

Meeting the conditions

Specific conditions must be met before a capital loss can be classified as a business investment loss. First, the shares or debt must be those of a small business corporation. Consult your tax adviser to determine if the corporation qualifies. In addition, if the loss results from an actual sale, you must have sold the shares or debt to a taxpayer not related to you. If the debt is established as a bad debt, you may recognize the loss even though a sale has not taken place (whether or not you are related to the corporation).

Similarly, if shares of a small business corporation are worthless, any capital loss incurred may qualify as a business investment loss. Your loss will be recognized, if you so elect, by filing a statement with your tax return, and if the following conditions apply. At the end of the year in which the loss is claimed, the company must be insolvent and not carrying on any business (together with any company it controls). Also, the fair value of the share must be nil and it must be reasonable to assume that the company will not commence carrying on a business and will be dissolved or wound up.

If you claim the loss and the company (or another company that it controls) begins to carry on a business within two years from the end of the year in which the loss was claimed, you will have to report a corresponding capital gain in the year the business commences.

Restrictions on ABILs

Following the introduction of the lifetime capital gains deduction, rules were introduced to prevent you from claiming the deduction and also benefiting from an allowable business investment loss (ABIL). The rules are similar to the restrictions placed on deductions for prior years' capital losses (see article 117). As a result, you will not be able to claim the capital gains deduction to the extent of ABILs claimed in 1985 or later.

It's a similar situation if you have claimed the capital gains deduction (on a disposition or as a result of the capital gains election) and you realize what would otherwise be an ABIL in a subsequent year. The loss will be treated as a regular allowable capital loss to the extent of your previously claimed capital gains deduction.

TAX TIP

If you have loaned money to a corporation and the debt is not collectible, consider whether you have incurred an ABIL. It is important that you determine when the amount becomes uncollectible. It's a definite plus to have a tax adviser in your corner if this situation arises.

119 Taxation of dividends

When you receive a dividend from a Canadian corporation, the amount you report on your return is not the amount you received—it's more. But this actually works to your advantage.

How are dividends taxed?

Dividends from taxable Canadian corporations are included in your income, along with a 25% gross-up of the amount received. You can then claim a federal dividend tax credit equal to 16 ⅔% of the actual dividend.

This tax credit reduces your federal income taxes. Each province has a similar mechanism to offset provincial income taxes.

As a result of this gross-up and tax credit mechanism, the effective rate of tax you pay on dividends is less than the rate you pay on most other sources of income. Depending on your province of residence, the top rate on Canadian dividend income is approximately 24% to 34% as opposed to roughly 39% to 49% on other sources of income (excluding capital gains) (see **Table 3**).

EXAMPLE
Dividend tax credit

If you received $1,000 of dividends from BCE Inc. in 2001, you must include $1,250 in your income. That makes you eligible to claim a federal tax credit of $167. Depending on the tax rates applicable to your particular province, you will pay a combined tax rate of 24% to 34% if you are in the top tax bracket (see **Table 3**). For example, if you live in Ontario, you will pay tax at an effective combined rate of 31.34% on the dividend. If you had received $1,000 of interest income (from bonds or GICs), you would have paid tax at an effective rate of 46.41%.

TAX TIP

If you have no other sources of income, you can receive approximately $25,000 in Canadian dividend income without paying any tax. The amount will vary depending on your province of residence at the end of the year.

Dividends received from a foreign corporation are not subject to the gross-up and tax credit mechanisms. Therefore, you will pay a higher rate of tax on this type of income (approximately 15% higher, depending on your province of residence).

Foreign spinoffs

In the past few years, you may have had to report foreign source dividend income when you received shares of a foreign corporation from another foreign corporation. This is called a spinoff transaction.

If the transaction was not taxable in the U.S., you may be able to make a special election that will allow you to avoid being taxed on the foreign source dividend for distributions received after 1997. For qualifying distributions received after 1997 and prior to the current year, the election had to be made by September 12, 2001. For distributions in current and future years, you must elect to take advantage of the deferral by including a letter with your tax return for the year in which the distribution occurs. This return must be paper filed with the CCRA.

To qualify for the deferral, the distribution of shares must be made by a widely held and actively traded U.S. public corporation. In addition, U.S. tax law must also provide for a tax deferral to the distributing corporation and its U.S. resident shareholders, and the foreign company that distributed the spin-off shares must provide specific information to the CCRA.

The new rules provide for a cost base adjustment to the original and spinoff shares based on their relative fair market values, as illustrated in the following example.

EXAMPLE

Cost base adjustment

Assume you own one original common share of AB Inc. (resident in the U.S.). AB Inc. distributes a spinoff share of CD Inc. (also resident in the U.S.) on a per-share basis to the holders of the common shares of AB Inc.

The cost amount of your original share in AB Inc. is $10 immediately before the distribution and its fair market value immediately after the distribution is $70. The fair market value of your CD Inc. spinoff share is $30 immediately after the distribution. The cost base of the original share ($10) must be reallocated to the original and spinoff shares as follows:

Original share	$10 × ($70 ÷ $100) = $7
Spinoff share	$10 × ($30 ÷ $200) = $3

Any gain or loss on a later sale of the original or spinoff shares would be the difference between the $7 or $3 calculated above and the net sale proceeds.

The government intends to prescribe other foreign countries as well. If you think you might qualify for a tax refund under these new rules, you should contact your tax adviser, who can assist you in making the special election.

120 Transfer of dividend income between spouses and common-law partners

If your spouse or common-law partner has little or no income except taxable dividends from Canadian corporations, you may reduce your family tax bill by including his or her dividends in your income.

This can only be accomplished if, by doing so, you are able to increase the claim you make for your spouse or common-law partner as a dependant. In effect, you delete the dividends from his or her income and include them in your income, entitling you to claim the dividend tax credit. The election must apply to all of your spouse or common-law partner's dividends from taxable Canadian corporations. You cannot pick and choose to maximize tax savings.

121 Taxation of interest income

A different set of rules is in place to determine when you must report interest income for tax purposes. Much of it depends on when the investment was purchased.

With the exception of certain investments made prior to 1990, you are required to report interest on investments on an annual basis, regardless of when the interest is actually paid. Similar rules apply to certain life insurance policies and annuity contracts. For investments purchased prior to 1990, you have the option of reporting interest income on either an annual accrual or three-year accrual basis.

You are also required to compute the interest on debt where the return on the investment is adjusted for inflation and/or deflation. If you own such a security, you will have to report an amount annually as interest income.

Do you own investments that earn significant interest income? There may be valid reasons for you to consider transferring them to a holding company—income splitting and estate planning, just to mention a couple. Proper planning is needed to ensure that the effects of the income attribution rules are minimized. Your tax adviser can assist you with this and can best assess if it's worth your while to do so.

122 Canada savings bonds

Reporting income earned on Canada savings bonds (CSBs) can be confusing because of the two different types of bonds available, regular or compound interest. With regular bonds, you will receive and report the interest each year. Compound bonds are another thing entirely. If you own compound bonds, you will not receive the interest until the bond matures or is cashed in. Nevertheless, the interest must now be reported annually. The three-year accrual rule (see article 121) was only available up to series 44 (issued in 1989), which matured in 1999. For compound bonds issued in 1990 and subsequent years, annual accrual is the only option available. The government will provide you with an information slip indicating the amount of income to be reported.

If you discover that you have not been reporting the interest on compound bonds properly, the tax department expects you to file amending information for the appropriate year.

When you purchase Canada savings bonds with a loan that is repaid through a payroll deduction plan, any interest you pay on the loan is deductible.

123 Mutual funds

Mutual funds are pools of assets that are invested by professional managers, either in general investments or in a particular individual sector.

Some mutual funds pay dividends, but may designate all or a portion of the dividends as capital gains dividends to reflect capital gains earned by the mutual fund. Such dividends are treated as capital gains and are generally subject to the usual capital gains treatment for income tax purposes.

Canadian mutual funds that invest in foreign companies are themselves considered Canadian property for the purposes of the foreign reporting rules (see article **132**).

Special rules apply if a capital gains election was made on a mutual fund (see article **112**). The capital gain elected does not increase the cost base of the mutual fund. Instead, a special tax account is created, called an "exempt capital gains balance." The balance in this account can be used to offset future capital gains designated by the fund, as well as any gain on actual disposition of the mutual fund units. In general, this account may be used within a 10-year period, and any balance remaining at the end of the year 2004 will be added to the cost base of the fund.

EXAMPLE

Capital gains in action

Let's say you made a $10,000 capital gains election in 1994 in respect of your mutual fund. In the following years, the fund designates capital gains paid to you as follows:

1995	$1,800
1996	1,500
1997	2,000
1998	1,000
1999	500
2000	2,000
	$8,800

You could use the $10,000 exempt capital gains balance created in 1994 to offset the allocated gains and you would still have an exempt capital gains balance of $1,200 remaining at the end of 2000 to shelter future gains from this mutual fund. For example, if you sold the mutual fund units in 2001 for a capital gain of $3,000, you could use your remaining balance to offset $1,200 of the gain.

> **TAX TIP**
>
> The amount of exempt capital gains balance claimed in a particular year is optional, up to the amount of the capital gains designated to you by the fund or the gain on disposition. In some cases, it may pay to claim other available deductions and credits.

What if you dispose of all your interests in your mutual fund at a loss and you still have a balance remaining in your exempt capital gains balance pool? In this situation, any unused balance in the account at that time may be added to the adjusted cost base of those interests or shares. This will give recognition to the appropriate capital loss on the disposition of the mutual fund units or shares.

> **TAX TIP**
>
> If you made a capital gains election on a mutual fund you have since disposed of, you should review your tax return to determine if there was any remaining exempt capital gains balance. If a balance was remaining, you should request an adjustment to the capital gain or capital loss reported. This applies to 1994 and subsequent years. Discuss the potential adjustment and tax savings with your tax adviser.

Capital gains distributed by a mutual fund trust

Private corporations can add the non-taxable portion of any capital gains realized to a special account called the capital dividend account. Dividends can be paid out of this account to shareholders on a tax-free basis.

For several years, it has been the CCRA's position that capital gains distributed by a mutual fund trust do not result in an addition to a corporation's capital dividend account. The Income Tax Act has recently been amended to correct this inequity—the non-taxable portion of capital gains distributed by a mutual fund trust can now be added to the computation of the capital dividend account. This amendment applies to elections in respect of capital dividends that became payable after 1997.

> **TAX TIP**
>
> If you are a shareholder of a corporation that invests in mutual funds, contact your tax adviser to determine if these new rules affect you. The rules in this area are complex and professional advice is a must.

124 Investment holding companies

The tax system contains special rules that are intended to eliminate any preference for earning income in a corporation as opposed to personally (see article **21**). Some of these are designed to ensure that the after-tax return on income realized through a corporation and subsequently distributed to the shareholder is roughly the same as if the shareholder had received the income from the investments directly.

Nevertheless, you might still want to use a company to hold your investments in some situations. For example, individuals eligible for OAS benefits whose personal income (excluding investment income) is roughly $55,000 or less may come out ahead by holding their investments in a corporation. Also, the largest deferral opportunities remain with dividend-producing assets, rather than interest. Investment holding corporations can also be used to implement an estate freeze (see article **107**).

Every situation is unique and requires a separate analysis. Your tax adviser can assist you in determining if this strategy is suitable for your particular situation.

TAX TIP

A regular review of your tax situation, including an annual look at your portfolio, is the best way to determine the most advantageous structure in light of any tax rate changes, new legislation, and changes to your business.

125 Demutualization—shares or cash?

Several Canadian life insurance companies have completed the demutualization process—the process of converting a mutual insurance company to a publicly traded company owned by its shareholders.

When such a company is demutualized, you will be given two choices. You can either receive a cash payment for the value of your existing investment or you can choose to receive a specified number of shares in the new company. The tax treatment afforded each option differs.

If you elect to take the cash settlement, the amount you receive is taxed as a dividend in the year you receive the payment. No income tax will be withheld at source, so you will pay the tax owing when you file your tax return for the year. If you opt to receive shares, you will not have any tax implications until you sell the shares. The shares will have a cost base of nil. Therefore, the sales proceeds will be taxed as a capital gain in the year you sell the shares.

Is it better to receive cash or shares? Owning shares in a company is always risky. There is no guarantee that the shares will increase in value. You must also consider that they can decrease in value. In making your decision, you should assess many factors—your financial situation, your financial goals and objectives, and your tolerance for risk.

126 Cumulative net investment loss rules

The rules governing the cumulative net investment loss (CNIL) were introduced in 1988 to prevent individuals from reducing their income by claiming investment losses, such as rental losses and carrying charges, and subsequently recouping the losses by selling the underlying investment and then not paying any tax on the resulting gain due to the capital gains deduction.

The elimination of the $100,000 capital gains deduction on other property means your CNIL will only be relevant for years after 1994 if you have a gain from the disposition of qualified farm property or a share of a qualified small business corporation.

What is a CNIL?

Your CNIL account is the cumulative excess of your investment expenses over your investment income. Investment expenses include losses from rental property, non-active partnership losses such as tax shelters, interest on money borrowed for investments, and 50% of resource-related deductions.

Investment income includes all income from property (including rental income, interest income, and dividends), non-active partnership income, and 50% of natural resource income. Investment income does not include taxable capital gains, although capital gains that cannot be sheltered by the capital gains deduction reduce the impact of the CNIL account.

Since the CNIL account is a cumulative account (for 1988 and subsequent years), it is recommended that you keep a running total each year even if you are not claiming a capital gains deduction in the year. In general, you will only be able to claim the capital gains deduction to the extent your taxable capital gain for the given year exceeds the amount of your CNIL.

TAX TIP

If you are an owner-manager of a corporation and have a CNIL problem, you should consider receiving enough interest or dividend income from your corporation to eliminate your CNIL.

TAX TIP

Where possible, borrow for business purposes as opposed to investment purposes. The interest expense on funds borrowed to carry on a business or profession does not enter into the calculation of your CNIL account.

127 Deductibility of interest expense

Interest expense is deductible for income tax purposes, provided the borrowed funds were used to earn income and certain other conditions are met. Over the years, the tax department has allowed interest as a deduction even though it may not be deductible from a strictly technical point of view—for instance, if a company borrows funds to pay a dividend rather than using its own funds. However, following a 1987 Supreme Court decision, considerable uncertainty developed as to whether interest would continue to be deductible under these circumstances.

When is interest deductible?

To try to resolve this problem, the government introduced draft legislation in 1991 regarding the deductibility of interest expense. These proposed changes deal with the deductibility of interest where borrowed money is used by corporations and partnerships to distribute retained earnings or capital.

Also included are provisions for borrowings made by shareholders and partners to loan money to a corporation or partnership or to honour a guarantee of its indebtedness. Borrowings used to acquire shares, and to make interest-free or low-interest loans to shareholders or employees, are also covered.

A fixed date has still not been set for the implementation of any of these changes, and the tax department has noted that it intends to follow current assessment practices until the final legislation is formally introduced. In general, interest will be deductible if the funds were borrowed to pay dividends or redeem shares, provided the amount of the dividend or redemption does not exceed the accumulated profits of the company.

Funds borrowed by individual shareholders to loan to their corporation at no interest or low interest will continue to be deductible. But, as usual, there is a catch. The funds must be used by the company to earn income, no unfair advantage can be derived, and the company cannot obtain the same terms of financing from a third party without the individual's guarantee.

As final or new legislation could be introduced at any time and current assessment practices are subject to change, you should check with your tax adviser to determine the CCRA's position if you are borrowing funds for any of these purposes.

What if you no longer own income-producing property?

During the 1980s, a series of cases stressed the link between a source of income and the related interest expense. The courts established that, where a source of income disappeared, the deductibility of interest on money borrowed to acquire the source ceased.

For example, if money was borrowed to acquire shares, and the shares were subsequently sold at a loss or were lost due to the bankruptcy of the company, the interest ceased to be deductible. There are now rules that may permit a continued deduction for interest expense, but they are complex and professional tax advice is recommended.

TAX TIP

When you borrow, try to borrow for investment or business purposes before you borrow for personal reasons. Conversely, when repaying debt, consider repaying loans on which interest is non-deductible before you repay those on which the interest is deductible. After all, why would you prematurely eliminate an arrangement that provides a measure of tax relief?

Was the real purpose a capital gain?

In one recent court case dealing with interest deductibility, taxpayers borrowed funds to acquire common shares in offshore corporations, disposed of their shares after several years, and reported substantial capital gains.

Although the deductibility of interest with respect to funds used to acquire common shares is generally not an issue, the taxpayers were not allowed to deduct their interest expense. The government took the position that the borrowed funds had not been used to earn income from a business or property, and that the taxpayers had no reasonable expectation of profit from the dividend payments. The real purpose of the investment was to realize a capital gain on their investment. The Federal Court of Appeal confirmed the decision of the lower court—interest is only deductible where the real or true purpose of using the borrowed money is to earn income. The Supreme Court has recently heard the appeal to this case and the decision is pending.

This case is significant in that taxpayers may now be required to demonstrate that they expected to earn reasonable income from their investments. If they cannot demonstrate this, then any interest expense incurred could be considered non-deductible. Although this decision reinforces the CCRA's position that interest on funds borrowed to realize a capital gain is not deductible, it also raised concerns about interest deductibility with respect to borrowings for common shares and other growth investments. In response, the tax department has stated that they will continue to permit a deduction for interest paid on funds borrowed to purchase most common shares.

128 Resource sector as a tax shelter

Most investors do not invest directly in the resource sector. Rather, they obtain tax writeoffs by investing in limited partnerships created for that purpose or by investing in shares of companies (flow-through shares) whereby the companies pass on the deductions to the shareholders, who claim them on their own tax returns.

You can currently claim four main types of resource expenses: Canadian development expenses (CDE), Canadian exploration expenses (CEE), Canadian oil and gas property expenses (COGPE), and foreign exploration and development expenses (FEDE). Each is subject to special rules regarding the amount you can claim as a deduction. As with any other investment, your decision to invest in the resource sector should be based on its overall investment potential, rather than just focusing on the writeoffs. Your financial adviser can help you make this assessment.

129 Limited partnerships

Another type of tax shelter involves the purchase of an interest in a limited partnership. In this type of arrangement, you share the profits or loss of the business with the other partners and report a percentage of the partnership's income or loss directly as your income or loss. However, your liability with respect to the partnership's debts is limited. In general, you can only lose up to your original investment.

Restrictions

Although a limited partnership may be an attractive investment if the partnership business is expected to have losses in its initial years but to show a profit eventually, special rules prevent you from writing off more than the amount you have invested in the partnership.

The writeoff you may claim is further restricted if the purchase of an interest is financed with certain types of "limited recourse" financing. Recent changes will also require certain partnerships to prorate expenditures that would otherwise be deductible in the current year over a longer term. In addition, if the adjusted cost base of your interest in a limited partnership becomes negative, you will have to report a capital gain equal to the negative amount. Along with other changes, these have substantially reduced the attractiveness of limited partnerships as a tax shelter.

As you would with any other investment, you should thoroughly evaluate the investment potential of a tax shelter. It does not make any economic sense to invest in a shelter if there is little chance of either earning a return on your investment or recovering the amount you have at risk.

The alternative minimum tax (AMT) (see article 133) and CNIL rules (see article 126), as well as restrictions on the deductibility of limited partnership losses, make it imperative that you pursue expert tax advice about your situation before making an investment.

130 Taxation of trusts

A trust is an arrangement under which a trustee holds property for the benefit of one or more beneficiaries. It can be created at any time, including on death through your will. Trusts are taxed as separate taxpayers. A trust created on death is taxed at the same rate as an individual, while other trusts are taxed at the highest marginal individual rate of tax (from 39% to about 49%, depending on the province in which the trust is taxed; see **Table 3**).

Flexibility in taxation

The income of the trust will be subject to tax, but exactly who gets taxed is flexible. If the trust agreement requires that the income be paid to beneficiaries, the general rule is that they pay the tax. However, it is possible to elect to have some or all of the income taxed in the trust. Alternatively, the trust agreement can provide that the income stays in the trust for a set period. In this case, the general rule is that the trust will pay the tax.

TAX TIP

Consider revising your will to create separate testamentary trusts for each of your beneficiaries. This will help them save tax on income they will earn on money you plan to leave them in your will.

The preferred-beneficiary election allows the trustee and the beneficiary to retain the income in the trust while having that income taxed in the hands of the beneficiary. This election is available only if the beneficiary is entitled to claim a tax credit because of a mental or physical impairment, and applies only to the beneficiary's share of the trust income.

TAX TIP

Consider creating a trust to hold investments for the benefit of a child or parent with a physical or mental disability. The income can be retained in the trust and may be taxed at a lower rate. This can effectively reduce taxes while allowing the trustee to control the investments.

The 21-year rule

Along with the introduction in 1972 of the tax on capital gains came the 21-year rule that prevents the indefinite deferral of tax on accrued gains on property held in trusts. Under this rule, every 21 years, most trusts are deemed to dispose of all of their property for proceeds equal to the fair market value of the property.

Just before the first disposition of property under the 21-year rule would have take place in 1993, the government responded to pressure to provide relief from this provision. In certain circumstances, a trustee was permitted to elect a deferral of the rule's application.

The government subsequently took a second look at this matter and decided that either the 21-year rule would be applied to tax accrued gains in 1993 or that the gains would be deemed to have been realized on January 1, 1999. If the trustee revoked the earlier election before 1997, the gains would be taxed in 1993. If not revoked, the deemed disposition took place on January 1, 1999.

TAX TIP

If you are the trustee of a trust that will soon be subject to the 21-year rule, contact your tax adviser to determine what strategies are available to avoid or defer the tax on the deemed disposition. If the trust document permits, it might be advantageous to transfer the capital property with the accrued gains to the capital beneficiaries.

131 Foreign taxes on investment income

As a resident of Canada, you are subject to Canadian income taxes on all your income, even if it was earned in another country. Along with interest or dividend income received from a foreign source, you must also declare as income the total of foreign taxes withheld. The foreign income is to be converted into Canadian dollars by using the average rate of exchange for 2001 or the actual exchange rate in effect when you received the income.

Foreign tax credits

You can claim a foreign tax credit for taxes withheld by the foreign country. In most cases, if the amount of foreign taxes withheld exceeds 15% of such income, the excess cannot be claimed as a foreign tax credit, though you may be able to deduct the excess tax paid as an expense against that foreign income. The foreign tax credit is calculated on a per-country basis, and separate calculations are required for business and non-business income tax.

TAX TIP

If you are a U.S. citizen who is resident in Canada, the impact of the tax department's position on assessing foreign tax credits could be substantial. U.S. citizens resident in Canada should therefore review the possible effects with their tax adviser.

132 Foreign reporting requirements

Many offshore investment vehicles rely on the fact that the taxpayer's interest in the offshore entity is not known to the Canadian authorities, but the government is aware of this shortcoming and is taking steps to correct the situation. The first step is to induce taxpayers to comply with the Canadian tax system and, to that end, foreign reporting requirements have been introduced.

What to report

Reporting may be required if a taxpayer has transferred or loaned funds or property to a foreign-based trust, received funds or property from or is indebted to a foreign-based trust, or has a foreign affiliate. Failure to disclose the required information may result in substantial penalties.

Loans and transfers to foreign trusts

If a taxpayer has transferred or loaned funds or property to a foreign-based trust at any time before the end of the trust's tax year, form T1141 must be filed by the due date for the taxpayer's return for the particular year that includes the end of the trust's year before which a transfer was made, or during which the non-resident trust was indebted to the taxpayer. For example, a corporation with a March 31 year-end transfers property to a foreign-based trust on June 30, 2000. The year-end of the trust is July 31. Since the March 31, 2001, year-end of the corporation includes the July 31, 2000, year-end of the trust—the year-end of the trust during which the transfer was made—form T1141 must be filed by September 30, 2001, which is the filing due date for the corporation's 2001 tax return.

Distributions by and loans from foreign trusts

If a taxpayer has received funds or property from, or is indebted to, a foreign-based trust, form T1142 must be filed by the due date of the taxpayer's tax return for the particular year during which a distribution was received, or during which the taxpayer was indebted to the foreign-based trust. In the case of a partnership, the form must be filed by the due date for the partnership information return, whether or not such a return is required. For example, an individual receives a distribution of funds from a trust on June 30, 2001. Form T1142 must be filed by the due date of the individual's 2001 tax return—either April 30, 2002, or June 15, 2002.

Interest in foreign affiliates

Taxpayers who own shares of foreign affiliates are also required to file an information return annually. The information return—form T1134-A or T1134-B, as appropriate—must be filed no later than 15 months after the end of the taxation year for which it is filed. For example, a corporation with a December 31, 2000, year-end is required to file this information return no later than March 31, 2002.

Foreign property holdings

Taxpayers with interests in certain foreign property (shares, bank accounts, real property, etc.) in excess of $100,000 must report and provide details of such holdings on form T1135. This form must be filed by the due date for filing the income tax return for the particular year. Certain foreign property, such as personal-use property and property that is used in carrying on an active business, is excluded from this reporting requirement.

For example, an individual owns a rental property in the United States that cost Cdn$150,000. Form T1135 must be filed by the due date of the individual's 2001 tax return—either April 30, 2002, or June 15, 2002.

TAX TIP

Does your portfolio include foreign investments? Then it's time to consult with your tax adviser to review filing requirements. In some cases, the information you are required to report will not be readily available and time will be needed to accumulate it. Failure to comply with these requirements can result in penalties.

133 Alternative minimum tax

The purpose of the alternative minimum tax (AMT) is to restrict the tax benefits derived from various tax preference items, such as approved tax shelters, capital gains, investment tax credits, and others. It either imposes an overall limit on the total of these identified deductions, credits, and exclusions, or reduces the tax savings derived from these items.

You should not have to pay any AMT unless your tax preference items exceed a $40,000 exemption. Even then, depending on your circumstances, the total of such items may go significantly beyond this limit before the AMT is triggered. In many cases, no AMT will be due. Additionally, it does not apply in the year of death.

Before 1998, pension deductions were also considered a "tax preference" item for purposes of this tax calculation. However, for 1998 and subsequent years, contributions to an RRSP or RPP will not have an impact on AMT, even if the contribution is larger than normal, such as could be the case if you received a retiring allowance.

EXAMPLE

The AMT calculation

For 2001, the AMT is calculated as 16% of the amount by which your "adjusted taxable income" exceeds the $40,000 exemption. Your adjusted taxable income is your taxable income determined for ordinary tax purposes adjusted to add back certain deductions ("tax preference items") that are not allowed as deductions for determining the AMT.

If your AMT exceeds the amount of your regular federal taxes payable, the AMT becomes the amount of federal tax used to determine your tax liability. From this amount, you subtract the tax credits (i.e., personal tax credit, spousal amount, etc.) that are allowable for AMT purposes and make all other necessary tax calculations (i.e., surtaxes, other credits, and provincial taxes).

Relief in future years

If you have to pay any AMT, you will pay more tax than required under the regular rules. However, you are entitled to a credit for the excess in future years when your regular tax liability exceeds your AMT for that year. The carry-forward period is seven years, and each year's credit cannot reduce your liability below your AMT amount for that year.

Everyone

This final section of *Smart Tax Tips* deals with topics that are endemic to most taxpayers—whether you are a business owner, aspiring entrepreneur, employee, homemaker, retiree, or anyone else who has to file an income tax return—especially if there are taxes owing.

Here we present a baker's dozen of items for your consideration. Some provide a bit of insight into how the tax department works, what it expects you to do, and what it will do if you can't comply. We concisely explain the CCRA's collection procedures, the penalties and interest you can expect, and the approaches you can use to mitigate the situation to the satisfaction of both parties.

This section also discusses how you can file your tax return electronically via EFILE, as well as a few other options available to some taxpayers.

134 Understand the rules before you act

Considering a financial transaction that is not part of your ordinary routine? It stands to reason that you should be up on all of the tax rules that apply. For the most part, taxation in Canada is quite complex, creating challenges for even the most knowledgeable. Often, you will discover there is more than one way to accomplish a particular goal and the tax impact may be radically different, depending on how you structure the transaction.

> **TAX TIP**
>
> In most cases, the opportunities available to save or defer income taxes arise at the preliminary stage, before you have completed the proposed transaction. The manner in which a transaction is structured may also affect the GST/HST payable. Having your tax adviser review what you have done after you have completed the arrangement is usually too late. The only way to take advantage of the rules is to conduct your tax planning well in advance.

▣ The CCRA'S policy and what's really law

In most cases, amendments to the Income Tax Act are presented to the House of Commons as part of a budget. The Department of Finance, under the direction of the Minister of Finance, prepares these amendments. Once they become law, the Canada Customs and Revenue Agency (CCRA) administers them.

Over the years, the tax department has developed a plethora of administrative rules in an effort to deal with practical problems that always seem to arise and the apparent uncertainty in many areas of tax law. In some cases, the administrative rules may not even agree with the law.

In tax planning, you should know whether your plan complies with the tax law or whether it depends on the tax department's stated policy. The CCRA is not bound by its stated policy, and the courts do not necessarily consider this policy in making their decisions.

▣ T4s, T5s, and other information slips

Any employment, pension, and most investment income you receive in 2001 is reported on information slips prepared by the person or organization that paid you. In general, these slips must be mailed or delivered to you by February 28, 2002.

If you are a beneficiary of a trust, your T3 information slip could be delayed until the end of March depending upon the year-end of the trust. Partnerships in which all of the members are individuals are required to file a partnership information return and issue the required information slips to the partners by March 31, 2002 (see article 3).

Whether you receive the appropriate slip or not, you must declare all your income. Be sure to check the amounts reported on the slips to ensure they are correct, as mistakes on these documents are not uncommon. If there is an error, you can obtain an amended slip. If you are filing your tax return on paper, do not file it until all the necessary receipts and slips are in your hands. Otherwise, processing delays could result. Nevertheless, you should do everything possible to ensure that you do not file late.

If you are filing your return electronically (see article 137), or using TELEFILE or NETFILE (see article 138), you must retain all information slips in case the CCRA requests confirmation of the amount claimed. Your return will be reassessed if you cannot provide a copy of the relevant slip.

▨137▨ Electronic filing of tax returns

Electronic filing (EFILE) is a system that allows authorized persons to send personal income tax returns directly to the CCRA over the telephone lines. Since the returns are received and verified almost instantly, refunds can often be issued within a couple of weeks of submitting your return.

The CCRA has also redesigned the corporate income tax system to facilitate electronic filing. Under this new system, previous forms and schedules have been revised and renumbered, and a uniform system of reporting financial information—the general index of financial information (GIFI)—has been introduced.

The GIFI is an index of items commonly found on income statements, balance sheets, and statements of retained earnings. Financial information will be submitted to the CCRA using this standard codified index, which will have to be used to EFILE a corporate tax return. GIFI is mandatory for all corporate tax returns with a year-end after 1999. Electronic filing of corporate tax returns is not yet mandatory, although its implementation is expected in the near future.

▨138▨ NETFILE and TELEFILE for individuals

For the past few years, selected individuals have been able to file their personal income tax return using the Internet. If you qualify to use this option, a unique numeric identifier called a "Web access code" is noted on the computer-generated label you receive from the CCRA. To file your return using the Internet, you must use a certified commercial tax software program that supports this function.

Also, since 1997, a telephone-based system for filing individual income tax returns called TELEFILE has been in use. Under this system, you can transmit income tax information yourself over the telephone. TELEFILE is available for taxpayers who file returns identified as T1S-A, T1S-B, T1S-C, or T1 Special (wage earners, students, seniors, and credit and benefit filers). It is also available to selected taxpayers who have previously filed their returns using computer software. The type of return you receive is based on your previous income tax filing information. If you are eligible to use TELEFILE, you will receive information about TELEFILE with your income tax package, as well as a personalized access code.

TELEFILE does not eliminate the need to complete a copy of the tax return. To use this system, you must enter data from a completed income tax return using your telephone keypad. On completion of the automated telephone interview, the CCRA will issue a confirmation number. A Notice of Assessment is usually sent out within two weeks.

Under both NETFILE and TELEFILE, you are not required to file the supporting documentation used to prepare the return unless requested to do so.

139 Notice of Assessment and your return

Within a few months of filing your 2001 return, you should receive a Notice of Assessment from the CCRA. When you receive it, compare it to the taxes payable as reported on your return. If there is any discrepancy, try to determine the reason.

If you do not understand why the amounts are different or you disagree with the assessment, consult your tax adviser or ask the CCRA to provide further details. Do not automatically assume you made the error. The assessment may be based on a misunderstanding of the facts, or the tax department quite possibly may have made an error in processing your return.

Reassessments and notices of objection

As a matter of policy, the CCRA will reassess returns if the adjustment relates to an error in arithmetic or a misunderstanding of the facts. If your dispute is based upon a different interpretation of the law, you have to file a notice of objection.

Taxpayers can initiate the appeal process by outlining the objection on form T400A or by setting out the facts and reasons for their objection in a letter to the chief of appeals at their local district taxation office.

Generally, a notice of objection must be filed within 90 days of the mailing date of the Notice of Assessment. Individuals and testamentary trusts are granted a longer period to object to their assessment. They must object within one year from the filing due date of the return or 90 days after the day of mailing the Notice of Assessment, whichever is later. Consult with your tax adviser if you believe a reassessment or an objection is warranted.

▐140▌ The fairness package

There are rules designed to improve the fairness of the tax system when personal misfortune or circumstances beyond your control make you unable to meet your filing or payment deadlines or comply with certain rules. For example, interest and penalties may be waived if you can show that you were prevented from filing on time due to extraordinary circumstances. These may include factors such as illness, death, natural disaster, disruption in services, or erroneous information from the tax department in the form of incorrect written answers or errors in published information.

Individuals and testamentary trusts can also use these rules to apply for a refund in respect of a prior year that would otherwise be statute-barred. Still other provisions permit you to amend or file certain prescribed tax elections late.

To request this relief, you must write a letter to the CCRA indicating why you think the fairness rules should apply to your particular situation and submit receipts or other backup information to support your claim. Relief is not automatic, and the rules are not intended to permit retroactive tax planning. However, the CCRA will generally permit the requested amendment where their guidelines have been met. Your tax adviser can assist you in determining whether you are likely to qualify, as well as in making the application.

▐141▌ The CCRA's collection procedures

If you cannot afford to pay taxes owing, you should know about the CCRA's collection procedures. Without a doubt, you should still file your return on time even if you are unable to pay the outstanding taxes. Filing late will incur a 5% penalty on the taxes owing, which is automatically added to the amount you owe. An additional 1% is added for each additional complete month that the return is late, to a maximum of 12 months. Interest also accrues on the unpaid taxes. And if this is not your first late filing offence and a demand has been issued for you to file a return, you could be subject to a 10% penalty plus 2% per month for up to 20 months on the second late-filed return. If you willfully attempted to evade payment of income taxes by failing to file your return, additional penalties could apply.

What to expect

Your Notice of Assessment will show the amount of taxes owing, including penalties and interest, and will state that no further interest will be charged if the entire amount is paid within 20 days. If a payment is not made within 30 days, the CCRA will issue a request that the amount be paid. In most cases, the CCRA cannot begin legal proceedings to collect until 90 days after the date of assessment. There are further delays if you file a notice of objection. Nevertheless, the daily-compounded interest is charged and accumulates on the amount due from April 30 to the date of payment.

Subject to the restrictions relating to disputed amounts, the CCRA can seize funds from your bank account or require your employer to pay a portion of your salary directly towards your taxes owing.

Try to work out a payment schedule

The CCRA will make every effort to contact you before beginning formal legal proceedings, but it would be prudent for you to contact the department if you are unable to pay the full amount immediately. Depending on circumstances, the tax department normally accepts a schedule of payments over a period of time.

142 Income tax refunds

You are eligible for an income tax refund if the amount of income taxes withheld from or paid by you during the year exceeds the actual taxes you owe. Although you may look forward to receiving a tax refund, it is not always good planning to get one. If you get a refund, that means the government has been holding your money and not paying you interest on it for many months.

TAX TIP

If you expect to receive a refund after filing your return—for example, due to RRSP contributions and other deductions—you can apply to the CCRA to obtain permission to have your source withholdings reduced. In some cases, the TD1 form you file with your employer can be amended to provide for the reduced withholdings.

Requesting a refund for overpayment

Individuals and testamentary trusts can now claim a tax refund for taxation years as far back as 1985. For example, you may find that you failed to claim the "equivalent-to-married tax credit" (see article 73) in prior years, even though you were entitled to do so. By writing a letter to the department, and including any supporting documents, you can request a refund.

Losing interest

Although you won't be penalized for filing a return late when you are owed a refund, interest does not begin to accrue on the refund amount until you file the return. For individual tax returns, interest on tax refunds does not start to accrue until 45 days after the balance-due date (April 30) or 45 days after the actual filing date—if it is later.

If you have made an error and you actually owe money, late filing penalties will apply on the balance owing. Therefore, regardless of whether you owe money or are receiving a refund, you should always file your return on time.

143 Income tax instalments

Instalments for individuals

Historically, if you owe taxes each year when filing your return, there is a good chance you will be required to prepay your tax through quarterly instalments. Failing to remit the instalments on time can be costly. The CCRA charges interest on the deficient amounts as if you owed the money and, if this interest charge adds up to more than $1,000, a charge of 50% of the interest in excess of $1,000 is added. This can become quite expensive and should be avoided if possible.

Instalments are due on March 15, June 15, September 15, and December 15. The rules used to determine when an individual is required to remit instalments cause difficulties for many taxpayers—which is precisely why it's so important to understand the requirement to make instalments and the options available to do so.

Instalments are required if the difference between your combined federal and provincial tax and the amount of tax actually withheld at source was greater than $2,000 in either 1999 or 2000 and will be greater than $2,000 in 2001. This last test requires an estimate in advance of the actual calculation of 2001 tax.

Once it is determined that you are required to make instalment payments in 2001, you can choose from three options to calculate the amount of your instalment.

Under the first two options, you can base your instalments on your 2000 tax or on your estimate of your 2001 tax. If you choose the latter option, be careful. Underestimating your 2001 tax means the CCRA will charge you interest based on the higher instalment required.

With the third option, the CCRA calculates the amount of your instalment and sends you the calculation as a reminder. The government initiated this option to eliminate some of the confusion in this area. Unfortunately, the calculation notices look very much like requests to pay and have created confusion for many taxpayers.

This method uses your 1999 tax as the base for the first two instalments. For the last two instalments, the amounts are based on your 2000 tax, less whatever was required for the first two instalments. The final result will be total instalments equal to 2000 tax.

The major advantage in paying the amounts shown on the CCRA notices is that you will not be charged any instalment interest if you pay on time. The CCRA sends the instalment reminders in batches of two—in February for the March and June instalments, and in August for the September and December instalments.

TAX TIP

If you discover during the year that you should have been paying higher instalments, it is possible to catch up because the CCRA will credit interest on overpayments and apply that against interest deficiencies. For instance, if you remit $5,000 on March 15, and then discover just before the June 15 deadline that you should be remitting $6,000 each quarter, it would be prudent for you to remit $8,000 on June 15, $5,000 on September 15 and $6,000 on December 15. The end result will be that you were $1,000 short for the three months from March 15 to June 15 and $1,000 over for the next three months. The interest calculations for these two periods will offset each other, assuming the prescribed interest rate does not change over that period.

Instalments for corporations

In general, your corporation is not required to make instalments if its total tax liability for the current or preceding taxation year is $1,000 or less. In this case, the amount owing is paid on the balance-due day for the taxation year.

Once it is determined that your corporation is required to make monthly instalment payments, the instalment amount can be determined in one of three ways. Each instalment is due on the last day of each month of the taxation year.

Under the first two options, you can base your corporation's instalments on its "instalment base" for the immediately preceding year, or you can base them on your estimate of its tax liability for the current year. Again, if you choose the latter option, be careful. As with individuals, if you underestimate the amounts, the CCRA will charge non-deductible interest on the underpayments.

Under the third option, the first two instalments can be calculated as $1/12$ of the corporation's instalment base for its second preceding taxation year, and the next 10 instalments can be based on the instalment base for the immediately preceding taxation year, after deducting the first two instalments.

With the exception of Ontario, Quebec, and Alberta, the provinces have entered into tax collection agreements with the federal government under which the federal government administers and collects provincial income tax as part of the federal tax system. For these provinces, the instalment base includes both the federal and provincial tax liability. Ontario, Quebec, and Alberta administer their own systems and collect their own income taxes.

TAX TIP

Although the third option appears the most complex, it has the advantage of allowing two months after the year-end for the accumulation of information needed to determine the prior year's instalment base. For this reason, it is commonly used.

There are special rules where a corporation has undergone a corporate reorganization or where the instalment base year was less than 365 days.

144 Books and records

Individual taxpayers should keep their tax records for at least four years—this is approximately how long the CCRA can take to reassess a return—and preferably longer.

If you operate a business, you must keep your business records for a minimum of six years from the end of the last tax year to which they relate. If a return is filed late, the books and records must be kept for six years from the day the return is filed. Note that the minimum retention period is generally determined by the last tax year for which a record may be required for purposes of the Income Tax Act, not the year in which the transaction occurred and the record was created. For example, records supporting the acquisition and capital cost of investments and other capital property should be maintained until the day that is six years from the end of the last tax year in which such an acquisition could enter into any calculation for income tax purposes.

Books and records can only be destroyed earlier if you obtain written permission from the tax department. To get such permission, you can use Form T137, Request for Destruction of Books and Records, or you can apply in writing to your local tax services office. A written request, signed by the person directly affected or an authorized representative, should provide the following information:

- a clear identification of books, records, or other documents to be destroyed;
- the tax years for which the request applies;
- details of any special circumstances that would justify destroying the books and records at an earlier time than what is normally permitted; and
- any other pertinent information.

145 Director's liability

As a director of a corporation, you should be aware of your responsibility should the corporation fail to deduct and remit income taxes on payments to employees or on certain payments to non-residents. Directors can also be held liable for failure to collect and remit GST/HST.

Should the corporation fail to deduct and remit, you can be liable along with the corporation for paying the required amounts, including interest and penalties. However, you will not be held liable if you can demonstrate that you exercised a reasonable degree of care to prevent the failure of withholding and remitting.

Nevertheless, there have been several court cases where directors have been found liable. Often, the moneylender cuts off the line of credit to the business and, as a result, the withholding cannot be paid. Since the withholding is supposed to be in a trust account, this excuse is generally not sufficient to protect you from liability. As you might expect, ignorance is not an acceptable defence.

TAX TIP

Do not take your responsibility as a director lightly. If the corporation is in financial difficulty, you should take additional precautions to ensure that withholding taxes are remitted on a timely basis. Consider resigning if the corporation of which you are a director is in serious trouble. As an added precaution, consider registering your resignation with the appropriate corporate registry.

146 Be aware of penalties and interest

The concept of increased penalties for repeat offenders is now firmly entrenched in the Income Tax Act.

The penalty for filing a return late is 5% of the unpaid taxes plus an additional 1% for each complete month the return is late, up to a maximum of 12 months—a maximum penalty of 17%.

Additionally, if you have been assessed this penalty for one or more of the three prior years and the CCRA issues a demand to file the current year's return, it's a good idea to comply. The penalty for a repeat offence will be 10% of the unpaid taxes plus an additional 2% per month for a period up to 20 months—a maximum penalty of 50% (see article **141**).

Similarly, if you fail to report an amount for a given year and then fail to report another amount in one or more of three subsequent years, a special penalty equal to 10% of the amount you failed to report the second time will apply.

And don't forget the additional penalties imposed for failing to make the appropriate income tax instalments (see article **143**).

There are also penalties for failing to provide your SIN (social insurance number) or your BN (business number) or for failing to include the SIN or BN on an information slip that you have prepared. Partnerships and tax shelters are also subject to penalties for failure to file the required information returns.

Even bigger penalties

If you knowingly, or in circumstances amounting to gross negligence, make false statements or omit information from a return, a penalty of 50% of the tax that would otherwise have been incurred may be imposed. And if the CCRA finds that a false statement or omission amounts to tax evasion, a fine of 50% to 200% of the tax evaded may be imposed.

The interest rate charged on amounts owing to the CCRA is 2% higher than the rate the CCRA pays on refunds. The increased rate applies to all amounts owing to the CCRA, including unpaid taxes, instalments, and source deductions.

Voluntary disclosures

It is the tax department's policy not to impose penalties when a voluntary disclosure is made. If a taxpayer has never filed tax returns and the returns are then voluntarily filed, the taxpayer will be required to pay only the tax owing—with interest—on the reported incomes. If a taxpayer has given incomplete information in a return and subsequently submits the missing information, the taxpayer will be required to pay only the tax owing on the adjusted income, with interest.

To make a voluntary disclosure, you have to initiate the process. A disclosure is not considered voluntary if it arises when the CCRA has begun an audit or a request for information has been issued. Contact your tax adviser about initial contact with the tax department and the information to be provided.

Ministerial discretion to waive interest and penalties

In some cases, interest and penalties may have arisen due to no fault of your own. To deal with such inequities, there are rules that allow the minister to waive or cancel interest or penalties at any time, starting with the 1985 taxation year (see article **140**).

Civil penalties for misrepresentation by third parties

It's not only taxpayers who have to deal with the prospect of penalties—tax preparers and other persons are now faced with their possible imposition.

Two new penalties have recently been introduced: one for advising or participating in a false filing and the other for participation in a tax shelter or other tax-planning arrangement that includes a false statement or omission that may be used for tax purposes by another person.

For participating in a false filing, the penalty is the greater of $1,000 or 50% of the tax sought to be avoided (subject to a $100,000 maximum). For misrepresentations in a tax-planning or valuation activity, the penalty is the greater of $1,000 or the person's gross entitlements with respect to the arrangement. "Gross entitlements" are defined as all amounts a person is entitled to receive or obtain with respect to the activity.

The penalties will apply where a person knowingly makes (or participates in the making of) a false statement or omission that is used for tax purposes by another person, or where the person would have known had it not been for circumstances amounting to culpable conduct. "Culpable conduct" is defined as conduct that is equivalent to intentional acting, that shows an indifference as to whether the tax law is complied with, or that shows a willful or reckless disregard for the law.

PAYMENT AND FILING DUE DATES

Type of Return	Payment Due Date[1]	Filing Due Date
Individual income tax returns:		
Federal and provincial[2]		
• general	April 30	April 30
• self-employed[3]	April 30	June 15
• deceased	April 30[4]	April 30/June 15[5]
Corporate income tax returns:	End of:	End of:
Federal, Alberta, Ontario, and Quebec	2 months after *y/e[6]	6 months after y/e
Corporate capital tax returns:	End of:	End of:
Federal[7]	2 months after y/e[6]	6 months after y/e
British Columbia	184 days after y/e	184 days after y/e
Saskatchewan	6 months after y/e	6 months after y/e
Manitoba	6 months after y/e	6 months after y/e
Ontario[8]	2 months after y/e[6]	6 months after y/e
Quebec[8]	2 months after y/e	6 months after y/e
Nova Scotia	6 months after y/e	6 months after y/e
New Brunswick	6 months after y/e	6 months after y/e
Trust (estate) income tax returns:		
Federal	90 days after y/e	90 days after y/e
Quebec	90 days after y/e	90 days after y/e
Information returns:		
Partnership	N/A	March 31[9]
Tax shelter	N/A	Last day of February
Transactions with related non-residents	N/A	6 months after y/e
Foreign holdings:		
Transfers/loans to non-resident trusts	N/A	Filing due date of taxpayer's income tax return for the year[10]
Distributions from non-resident trusts	N/A	Filing due date of tax-payer's income tax return or partnership's information return[11]
Interests in foreign affiliates	N/A	15 months after y/e
Specified foreign property	N/A	Filing due date of tax-payer's income tax return or partnership's information return

Information slips:

T4, T5	N/A	Last day of February[12]
T3	N/A	90 days after y/e

* Note: (y/e means year-end)

1. The date indicates the due date for the final payment of taxes for the year. Instalment payments may be required throughout the year. Individuals, if required, make quarterly tax instalments (i.e., March 15, June 15, September 15, and December 15). Corporations, if required, generally remit taxes monthly.

2. Quebec is currently the only province that requires a separate individual tax return.

3. The filing deadline applies to an individual who carried on business (other than a tax shelter investment) in the year and his or her spouse or common-law partner.

4. For deaths occurring before November 1 of the year. For deaths occurring during November and December of the year, tax is payable six months after the date of death. When the death occurs between January 1 and April 30, the tax payable for the prior year is due six months after the date of death. Quarterly instalments of tax are not required after the date of death.

5. For deaths occurring before November 1 of the year, the return is due by the normal filing date, either April 30 or June 15. For deaths during the period beginning November 1 of the year and ending April 30 of the following year (or June 15 if the filing extension would have applied), the return is due by the later of six months after the date of death and the normal filing date.

6. End of third month following the y/e if the corporation is a Canadian-controlled private corporation and:

   Federal: the small business deduction is claimed in the current or preceding year, and the aggregate of taxable income of the corporation and all associated corporations for the immediately preceding year was $200,000 or less.

   Ontario: the corporation has taxable income for the preceding year of less than $200,000.

   Alberta: in either the current or the immediately preceding year have claimed the Alberta small business deduction and had taxable income of not more than $500,000.

7. Applies to large corporations and financial institutions capital tax. Separate capital tax returns are not required. Schedules are filed with the federal income tax return.

8. Part of the corporate income tax return. A separate tax return is not required.

9. If all members are individuals. If all members are corporations, the deadline is the last day of the fifth month following the fiscal year-end. For partnerships with mixed members, it is the earlier of these two dates. If the partnership discontinues its business or activity, the deadline is the earlier of 90 days after the discontinuance or the date the return would be required.

10. Where a taxpayer has transferred or loaned funds or property at any time to a foreign-based trust, the information return must be filed by the due date of the taxpayer's return for the particular year that includes the end of the trust's year before which a transfer was made, or during which the non-resident trust was indebted to the taxpayer.

11. Where a taxpayer or partnership has received funds or property from or is indebted to a foreign-based trust, the information return must be filed by the due date of the taxpayer's return for the particular year during which the distribution was received or the taxpayer was indebted to the foreign trust. In the case of a partnership, the information return must be filed by the due date of the partnership information return, whether or not one is required.

12. Where the business activity is discontinued, the filing deadline is 30 days thereafter.

These tax tables are a handy reference for federal tax credits, federal and provincial personal tax rates, corporate tax rates, and employment insurance rates. During the year, the federal and provincial governments occasionally revise these rates. To view the most up-to-date information, visit the Grant Thornton Web site at **www.GrantThornton.ca/smarttaxtips**.

Table I

2001 Federal Tax Credits

This table shows the amounts you can claim as credits and the approximate tax savings that correspond to each.

Type of credit	Amount ($)	Federal tax credit	Approximate tax saving (a)
Basic personal amount	$7,412	$1,186	$1,779
Married amount (b)	$6,294	$1,007	$1,511
Infirm dependants 18 and over (c)	$3,500	$560	$840
Disability (d) and (e)	$6,000	$960	$1,440
Caregivers' amount (f)	$3,500	$560	$840
Age 65 or over (d) and (g)	$3,619	$579	$869
Pension income (d)	up to $1,000	16% (up to $160)	24% (up to $240)
Tuition fees (d) (h) and (i)	amount paid (minimum $100 per institution)	16%	24%
Education (d) (h) and (i)			
—full-time	$400/month	16%	24%
—part-time	$120/month	16%	24%
Medical expenses	amount over lesser of $1,678 and 3% of net income	16%	24%
Student loan interest	amount paid	16%	24%
Charitable donations (j)	up to 75% of net income	16% of first $200; 29% of excess	24% of first $200; 43.5% of excess

CPP and UI premiums	limited to maximum premium for the year	16%	24%

The unused portion of any tax credits is not refundable to individuals who otherwise have no tax to pay.

Notes:

(a) Assumes the provincial tax rate is approximately 50% of the federal tax rate.

(b) Amount claimed for spouse or common-law partner, or equivalent-to-married credit for a related dependant. The value of the credit is reduced by 16% of the spouse's or common-law partner's (or dependant's) income in excess of $629.

(c) The value of the credit is reduced by 16% of the dependant's income in excess of $4,966.

(d) The unused portion of the credit is transferable as follows:

Age and pension income—to spouse or common-law partner only (see articles **81** and **82**)

Tuition fees/education—to spouse or common-law partner, or supporting parent or grandparent (see article **79**)

Disability—to spouse or common-law partner or other supporting person (see article **74**).

(e) The taxpayer is not entitled to this amount if medical expenses for a full-time attendant or for care in a nursing home have been claimed. In addition to the $6,000 amount, there is a $3,500 disability tax credit supplement for children with severe disabilities.

(f) The value of the credit is reduced by 16% of the dependant's income in excess of $11,953.

(g) The amount eligible for the credit (i.e., $3,619) is reduced by 15% of net income in excess of $26,941.

(h) The maximum transferable tax credit is $800 (tuition fees and education credit combined).

(i) Tuition and education amounts not fully used in the current year by the student and not transferred to an eligible person can be carried forward for the student's use in a subsequent year.

(j) In the year of death, the limit may be raised to 100% of net income. Special rules apply where capital property is donated to a charity (see article **75**).

Table 2

2001 Personal Income Tax Rates

Federal tax rates

Taxable income	Income tax
$30,754 or less	16%
$30,755 to $61,509	$4,921 + 22% on next $30,755
$61,510 to $100,000	$11,687 + 26% on next $38,491
Over $100,000	$21,695 + 29% on excess

Provincial tax rates

All of the provinces have now implemented a "tax on income" system that permits the province to levy its tax directly on taxable income rather than as a percentage of federal tax and gives it the flexibility to determine its own tax brackets and non-refundable credits.

Notes:

(a) British Columbia has five tax rates, as follows: 7.3% (up to $30,484); 10.5% ($30,485 to $60,969); 13.7% ($60,970 to $70,000); 15.7% ($70,001 to $85,000); and 16.7% (over $85,000). There are no surtaxes. The five proposed tax rates for the year 2002 are as follows: 6.05%; 9.15%; 11.7%; 13.7%; and 14.7%. The tax brackets will be indexed for provincial inflation.

(b) Alberta taxes all income at the rate of 10%. There are no surtaxes.

(c) Saskatchewan has three tax rates, as follows: 11.5% (up to $30,000); 13.5% ($30,000 to $60,000); and 16% (over $60,000). There are no surtaxes. The proposed rates for 2002 are 11.25%; 13.5%; and 15.5% (for the same income tax brackets as 2001). For 2003, the rates will be 11.5% on the first $35,000; 13% on the next $65,000; and 15% on the remainder.

(d) Manitoba has three tax rates, as follows: 10.9% (up to $30,544); 16.2% ($30,545 to $61,089); and 17.4% (over $61,089). There are no surtaxes. It is proposed that the three rates for 2002 will be 10.9%; 15.4% (reduced to 14.9% in 2003); and 17.4%.

(e) Ontario has three tax rates, as follows: 6.2% (up to $30,814); 9.24% ($30,815 to $61,629); and 11.16% (over $61,629). In addition, there is a surtax equal to 20% of Ontario tax over $3,560, plus 36% of Ontario tax over $4,491. It is proposed that effective January 1, 2002, the three rates will be 6.05%; 9.15%; and 11.16% (reduced to 5.65%; 8.85%; and

11.16% for 2003). The existing tax brackets will be indexed for inflation after 2001. It is also proposed that the first-tier surtax will be eliminated effective January 1, 2003. At that time, the surtax will equal 56% of Ontario tax over $4,491 (indexed after 2001).

(f) Quebec has three tax rates, as follows: 17% (up to $26,000); 21.25% ($26,001 to $52,000); and 24.5% (over $52,000). There are no surtaxes. It is proposed that the three rates for 2002 will be 16%; 20%; and 24%. The tax brackets will be indexed for inflation after 2001.

(g) New Brunswick has four tax rates, as follows: 9.68% (up to $30,754); 14.82% ($30,755 to $61,509); 16.52% ($61,510 to $100,000); and 17.84% (over $100,000). There are no surtaxes.

(h) Prince Edward Island has three tax rates, as follows: 9.8% (up to $30,754); 13.8% ($30,755 to $61,509); and 16.7% (over $61,509). In addition, there is a surtax equal to 10% of Prince Edward Island tax over $5,200. The low-income tax reduction is continued as a non-refundable tax credit based on family size and combined family income.

(i) Nova Scotia has three tax rates, as follows: 9.77% (up to $29,590); 14.95% ($29,591 to $59,180); and 16.67% (over $59,180). In addition, there is a surtax equal to 10% of Nova Scotia tax over $10,000.

(j) Newfoundland has three tax rates, as follows: 10.57% (up to $29,590); 16.16% ($29,591 to $59,180); and 18.02% (over $59,180). In addition, there is a surtax equal to 9% of Newfoundland tax over $7,032.

(k) The Yukon has four tax rates paralleling the federal tax brackets—7.36%; 10.12%; 11.96%; and 13.34%. There is a surtax equal to 5% of Yukon tax over $6,000.

(l) The Northwest Territories and Nunavut have four tax rates paralleling the federal tax brackets—7.2%; 9.9%; 11.7%; and 13.05%. There are no sur-taxes. It was originally proposed that the Northwest Territories would move to a "tax on income" system starting in 2003. However, on June 6, 2001, it was announced that the NWT would change to this system in 2001. Nunavut also moved to a "tax on income" system in 2001.

Table 3

2001 Top Marginal Rates of Tax

(federal and provincial combined)

Province	Interest and foreign dividends %	Canadian dividends %	Capital gains %
British Columbia	45.70	33.08	22.85
Alberta	39.00	24.08	19.50
Saskatchewan	45.00	29.58	22.50
Manitoba	46.40	33.83	23.20
Ontario	46.41	31.34	23.21
Quebec	48.72	33.44	24.36
New Brunswick	46.84	32.38	23.42
Prince Edward Island	47.37	31.96	23.69
Nova Scotia	47.34	31.92	23.67
Newfoundland	48.64	31.87	24.32
Yukon	43.01	29.04	21.50
Northwest Territories	42.05	28.40	21.03
Nunavut	42.05	28.40	21.03

Notes:

Interest and foreign dividends are taxed in the same way as most income. Canadian dividends are subject to a gross-up and a tax credit, producing a lower tax burden. Capital gains receive favourable treatment because only one-half of capital gains are taxed at the same rate as interest (three-quarters for gains realized before February 28, 2000, and two-thirds for gains realized after February 27, 2000, and before October 18, 2000).

Table 4

Tax Payable at Various Levels of Taxable Income (a)

Taxable income ($)	British Columbia		Alberta	
	tax ($)	percentage (%)*	tax ($)	percentage (%)*
20,000	2,890	23.3	2,724	26
22,000	3,356	23.3	3,244	26
24,000	3,822	23.3	3,764	26
26,000	4,288	23.3	4,284	26
28,000	4,754	23.3	4,804	26
30,000	5,220	23.3	5,324	29.7
32,000	5,809	32.5	5,919	32
34,000	6,459	32.5	6,559	32
36,000	7,109	32.5	7,119	32
38,000	7,759	32.5	7,839	32
40,000	8,409	32.5	8,479	32
42,000	9,059	32.5	9,119	32
44,000	9,709	32.5	9,759	32
46,000	10,359	32.5	10,399	32
48,000	11,009	32.5	11,039	32
50,000	11,659	32.5	11,679	32
52,000	12,309	32.5	12,319	32
54,000	12,959	32.5	12,959	32
56,000	13,609	32.5	13,599	32
58,000	14,259	32.5	14,239	32
60,000	14,909	32.5	14,879	33
62,000	15,611	39.7	15,538	36
64,000	16,405	39.7	16,258	36
66,000	17,199	39.7	16,978	36
68,000	17,993	39.7	17,698	36
70,000	18,787	41.7	18,418	36
75,000	20,872	41.7	20,218	36
80,000	22,957	41.7	22,018	36
85,000	25,042	42.7	23,818	36
90,000	27,177	42.7	25,618	36
95,000	29,312	42.7	27,418	36
100,000	31,447	45.7	29,218	39
105,000	33,732	45.7	31,168	39
110,000	36,017	45.7	33,118	39
115,000	38,302	45.7	35,068	39
120,000	40,587	45.7	37,018	39
125,000	42,872	45.7	38,968	39
150,000	54,297	45.7	48,718	39
250,000	99,997	45.7	87,718	39
500,000	214,247	45.7	185,218	39

* see note (b)

Taxable income ($)	Saskatchewan tax ($)	percentage (%)*	Manitoba tax ($)	percentage (%)*
20,000	3,394	27.5	3,386	26.9
22,000	3,944	27.5	3,924	26.9
24,000	4,494	27.5	4,462	26.9
26,000	5,044	27.5	5,000	26.9
28,000	5,594	27.5	5,538	26.9
30,000	6,144	33.2	6,076	26.9
32,000	6,809	35.5	6,766	38.2
34,000	7,519	35.5	7,530	38.2
36,000	8,229	35.5	8,294	38.2
38,000	8,939	35.5	9,058	38.2
40,000	9,649	35.5	9,822	38.2
42,000	10,359	35.5	10,586	38.2
44,000	11,069	35.5	11,350	38.2
46,000	11,779	35.5	12,114	38.2
48,000	12,489	35.5	12,878	38.2
50,000	13,199	35.5	13,642	38.2
52,000	13,909	35.5	14,406	38.2
54,000	14,619	35.5	15,170	38.2
56,000	15,329	35.5	15,934	38.2
58,000	16,039	35.5	16,698	38.2
60,000	16,749	39	17,462	38.2
62,000	17,528	42	18,257	43.4
64,000	18,368	42	19,125	43.4
66,000	19,208	42	19,993	43.4
68,000	20,048	42	20,861	43.4
70,000	20,888	42	21,729	43.4
75,000	22,988	42	23,899	43.4
80,000	25,088	42	26,069	43.4
85,000	27,188	42	28,239	43.4
90,000	29,288	42	30,409	43.4
95,000	31,388	42	32,579	43.4
100,000	33,488	45	34,749	46.4
105,000	35,738	45	37,069	46.4
110,000	37,988	45	39,389	46.4
115,000	40,238	45	41,709	46.4
120,000	42,488	45	44,029	46.4
125,000	44,738	45	46,349	46.4
150,000	55,988	45	57,949	46.4
250,000	100,988	45	104,349	46.4
500,000	213,488	45	220,349	46.4

Taxable income ($)	Ontario tax ($)	percentage (%)*	Quebec (c) tax ($)	percentage (%)*
20,000	2,794	22.2	3,281	30.4
22,000	3,238	22.2	3,888	30.4
24,000	3,682	22.2	4,495	30.4
26,000	4,126	22.2	5,102	34.6
28,000	4,570	22.2	5,795	34.6
30,000	5,014	22.2	6,487	35.8
32,000	5,568	31.2	7,241	39.6
34,000	6,193	31.2	8,034	39.6
36,000	6,818	31.2	8,826	39.6
38,000	7,443	31.2	9,619	39.6
40,000	8,068	31.2	10,411	39.6
42,000	8,692	31.2	11,203	39.6
44,000	9,317	31.2	11,996	39.6
46,000	9,942	31.2	12,788	39.6
48,000	10,567	31.2	13,581	39.6
50,000	11,192	31.2	14,372	39.6
52,000	11,816	31.2	15,164	42.9
54,000	12,448	33.1	16,022	42.9
56,000	13,109	33.1	16,879	42.9
58,000	13,771	33.1	17,737	42.9
60,000	14,433	33.1	18,594	42.9
62,000	15,124	39.4	19,468	46.2
64,000	15,937	43.4	20,392	46.2
66,000	16,805	43.4	21,314	46.2
68,000	17,673	43.4	22,238	46.2
70,000	18,542	43.4	23,165	46.2
75,000	20,712	43.4	25,475	46.2
80,000	22,883	43.4	27,787	46.2
85,000	25,053	43.4	30,096	46.2
90,000	27,223	43.4	32,407	46.2
95,000	29,394	43.4	34,717	46.2
100,000	31,564	46.4	37,028	48.7
105,000	33,885	46.4	39,463	48.7
110,000	36,206	46.4	41,899	48.7
115,000	38,526	46.4	44,335	48.7
120,000	40,847	46.4	46,770	48.7
125,000	43,167	46.4	49,205	48.7
150,000	54,770	46.4	61,381	48.7
250,000	101,179	46.4	110,093	48.7
500,000	217,203	46.4	231,875	48.7

Taxable income ($)	New Brunswick		Prince Edward Island	
	tax ($)	percentage (%)*	tax ($)	percentage (%)*
20,000	3,233	25.7	3,248	25.8
22,000	3,746	25.7	3,764	25.8
24,000	4,260	25.7	4,280	25.8
26,000	4,773	25.7	4,796	25.8
28,000	5,287	25.7	5,312	25.8
30,000	5,801	25.7	5,828	25.8
32,000	6,453	36.8	6,468	35.8
34,000	7,190	36.8	7,184	35.8
36,000	7,926	36.8	7,900	35.8
38,000	8,663	36.8	8,616	35.8
40,000	9,399	36.8	9,332	35.8
42,000	10,135	36.8	10,048	35.8
44,000	10,872	36.8	10,764	35.8
46,000	11,608	36.8	11,480	35.8
48,000	12,345	36.8	12,196	35.8
50,000	13,081	36.8	12,912	35.8
52,000	13,817	36.8	13,630	37.2
54,000	14,554	36.8	14,374	37.2
56,000	15,290	36.8	15,117	37.2
58,000	16,027	36.8	15,861	37.2
60,000	16,763	36.8	16,605	37.2
62,000	17,527	42.5	17,384	44.4
64,000	18,378	42.5	18,271	44.4
66,000	19,228	42.5	19,158	44.4
68,000	20,079	42.5	20,046	44.4
70,000	20,929	42.5	20,933	44.4
75,000	23,055	42.5	23,152	44.4
80,000	25,181	42.5	25,370	44.4
85,000	27,307	42.5	27,589	44.4
90,000	29,433	42.5	29,807	44.4
95,000	31,559	42.5	32,026	44.4
100,000	33,686	46.8	34,244	47.4
105,000	36,028	46.8	36,613	47.4
110,000	38,370	46.8	38,981	47.4
115,000	40,712	46.8	41,350	47.4
120,000	43,054	46.8	43,718	47.4
125,000	45,396	46.8	46,087	47.4
150,000	57,106	46.8	57,929	47.4
250,000	103,946	46.8	105,299	47.4
500,000	221,046	46.8	223,724	47.4

Taxable income ($)	Nova Scotia tax ($)	percentage (%)*	Newfoundland tax ($)	percentage (%)*
20,000	3,262	25.8	3,345	26.6
22,000	3,777	25.8	3,876	26.6
24,000	4,292	25.8	4,408	26.6
26,000	4,808	25.8	4,939	26.6
28,000	5,323	25.8	5,470	27.7
30,000	5,860	31	6,025	32.2
32,000	6,554	37	6,743	38.2
34,000	7,293	37	7,507	38.2
36,000	8,032	37	8,270	38.2
38,000	8,771	37	9,033	38.2
40,000	9,510	37	9,796	38.2
42,000	10,249	37	10,559	38.2
44,000	10,988	37	11,323	38.2
46,000	11,727	37	12,086	38.2
48,000	12,466	37	12,849	38.2
50,000	13,205	37	13,612	38.2
52,000	13,944	37	14,375	38.2
54,000	14,683	37	15,139	38.2
56,000	15,422	37	15,902	38.2
58,000	16,161	37	16,665	40.0
60,000	16,914	38.7	17,465	41.6
62,000	17,707	42.7	18,318	45.6
64,000	18,561	42.7	19,231	45.6
66,000	19,414	42.7	20,144	45.6
68,000	20,268	42.7	21,056	45.6
70,000	21,121	42.7	21,969	45.6
75,000	23,254	42.7	24,251	45.6
80,000	25,396	44.3	26,533	45.6
85,000	27,613	44.3	28,816	45.6
90,000	29,830	44.3	31,098	45.6
95,000	32,046	44.3	33,380	45.6
100,000	34,263	47.3	35,661	48.6
105,000	36,629	47.3	38,093	48.6
110,000	38,996	47.3	40,525	48.6
115,000	41,363	47.3	42,957	48.6
120,000	43,730	47.3	45,390	48.6
125,000	46,097	47.3	47,822	48.6
150,000	57,931	47.3	59,982	48.6
250,000	105,268	47.3	108,624	48.6
500,000	223,611	47.3	230,228	48.6

Notes:

(a) This table shows the amount of tax payable for a given taxable income by a person whose only tax credit is the basic non-refundable personal credit and who has no income from taxable Canadian dividends. Taxable income is assumed to be equal to net income.

(b) The marginal rate of tax is the average rate applicable to each additional $1 of income within the interval indicated on the table.

(c) Quebec's tax system is significantly different from those of the other provinces, and the amounts listed are illustrative rather than exact calculations. Allowable deductions will generally make taxable income somewhat lower for a taxpayer with the same total income who resides elsewhere in Canada.

In addition, individuals other than trusts are able to choose between the general tax system and a new, simplified income tax system. Opting for the simplified tax system, individuals replace a number of tax credits and deductions with a lump-sum non-refundable credit of $545.00 per taxpayer. Under this new system, spouses will also be able to file a joint return if they wish.

Table 5

Canada Pension Plan Contributions and Benefits (2001)

Contributions:	
Pensionable earnings	$38,300
Year's basic exemption	$3,500
Maximum contributory earnings	$34,800
Employee and employer rate	4.3%
Maximum annual employee/employer contribution	$1,496.40
Maximum annual self-employed contribution	$2,992.80

Benefits:	
Maximum monthly pension:	
if starting at age 60	$542.50
if starting at age 65	$775.00
if starting at age 70	$1007.50
Maximum single payment on death	$2,500.00
Maximum monthly pension for surviving spouse	
or common-law partner:	
under 65 years of age	$428.70
65 years of age and over	$465.00
Maximum monthly disability pension	$935.12

Notes:

(a) Persons over 60 years of age are eligible to receive pension benefits. The pension amount is reduced before age 65 or increased after age 65 by ½ of 1% (or 6% per year) for each month between the beneficiary's 65th birthday and the month the pension becomes payable. The contributor has the option of drawing retirement benefits as early as age 60 or as late as age 70.

(b) When the surviving spouse or common-law partner reaches 65, the pension is equal to 60% of the retirement pension.

(c) An individual who is married or living common-law can apply to have up to 50% of his or her CPP retirement benefits assigned to his or her spouse or common-law partner, provided the latter is at least 60 years old (see article 93). CPP credits may also be divided on application by a legal spouse or common-law partner after a separation of at least one year.

Table 6

Employment Insurance (2001)

Maximum insurable earnings	$39,000
Employee rate	2.25%
Maximum employee premiums	$877.50
Employer rate	3.15%
Maximum employer premiums	$1,228.50
Maximum weekly benefits	$413

Repayment of employment insurance (EI) benefits

You must repay a percentage of your EI benefits if your net income for the year exceeds a threshold amount. The repayment is 30% of the amount by which your net income exceeds $48,750. All first-time claimants, and EI special benefits for sickness, maternity, or parental reasons, are exempt.

The repayment must be included in your income tax return as taxes payable, and the amount is deductible in computing net income for the year.

Non-insurable employment:

- employment by a corporation of a person who owns more than 40% of the issued voting shares
- certain non-arm's-length employment
- casual employment if it is not for your usual trade or business

Table 7

2001 Federal Corporate Income Tax Rates plus Surtax

		with surtax
Income eligible for the small business deduction	12	13.12 (a)
Active business income of CCPC from $200,000 to $300,000	21	22.12 (b)
Active business income not eligible for the small business deduction—other business income	27	28.12 (c)
Active business income not eligible for the small business deduction—manufacturing and processing profits earned in Canada	21	22.12
Income not from an active business (CCPC)	28	29.12 (d)

Notes:

(a) Larger corporations' access to this rate is restricted. The restriction applies to CCPCs whose taxable capital exceeds $10 million for the preceding year. If the taxable capital is between $10 million and $15 million, the amount eligible for the low rate is reduced from the maximum of $200,000. Any eligibility ceases if taxable capital surpasses $15 million.

(b) Effective January 1, 2001, a CCPC can claim a 7% rate reduction on its active business income between $200,000 and $300,000 (on an associated group basis) (see article 22).

(c) The general corporate rate (before the 4% surtax) is 28%. This rate will be reduced to 21% by January 1, 2004, as follows: January 1, 2001 (27%); January 1, 2002 (25%); January 1, 2003 (23%); and January 1, 2004 (21%). This rate reduction does not apply to corporations that are not CCPCs, investment corporations, mortgage investment corporations, mutual fund corporations, or non-resident-owned investment corporations.

(d) A refundable tax of 6 ⅔% is imposed on investment income of a CCPC. This tax is in addition to the taxes outlined above and will be included as a portion of the taxes that may be refunded to a corporation on the payment of a taxable dividend.

2001 Provincial Corporate Tax Rates

	Small Business Deduction only	Manufacturing & Processing only	Other Income
British Columbia	0% or 4.5% (a)	16.5% (a)	16.5% (a)
Alberta	5% (b)	13.5% (c)	13.5% (c)
Saskatchewan	8% or 6% (d)	10%	17%
Manitoba	6% (e)	17%	17%
Ontario	6.5% (f)(g)	12% (h)	14% (i)
Quebec	0% or 8.9% (j)	8.9% (j)	8.9% or 16.25% (j)(k)
New Brunswick	4% (l)	16%	16%
Prince Edward Island	7.5%	7.5%	16%
Nova Scotia	0% or 5% (m)	16%	16%
Newfoundland	5%	5%	14%
Yukon	2.5% or 6% (n)	2.5%	15%
Northwest Territories	5%	14%	14%
Nunavut	5%	14%	14%

In addition to income tax, related corporations (associated corporations in the case of CCPCs) with aggregate taxable capital employed in Canada greater than $10 million are subject to a 0.225% federal large corporations tax (financial institutions may be subject to additional capital taxes). Most of the provinces also impose capital taxes on corporations that have permanent establishments in the province.

Notes:

(a) In B.C., there is a two-year corporate income tax holiday for eligible new small businesses incorporated after April 30, 1996, and before April 1, 2001. The small business tax holiday has not yet been extended. Effective January 1, 2002, the rate for M&P and Other Income will be reduced from 16.5% to 13.5%.

(b) The rate was reduced from 6% to 5%, effective April 1, 2001. Subject to affordability, the eligible income threshold for small businesses will double to $400,000 over two years and the small business rate will be reduced to 3% effective April 1, 2003.

(c) Effective April 1, 2001, the M&P rate was reduced from 14.5% to 13.5% and the rate on other income was reduced from 15.5% to 13.5%. Subject to affordability, the M&P and general rate will be reduced to 8% effective April 1, 2004.

(d) Effective July 1, 2001, the small business rate is reduced from 8% to 6%. The amount of income eligible for the small business rate will increase from $200,000 to $300,000 effective January 1, 2002.

(e) Rate reduced to 6% effective January 1, 2001. This applies to the first $200,000 of active business income. A further reduction to 5% will become effective on January 1, 2002, on the first $300,000 of active business income.

(f) Annual rate reductions each January 1 will reduce the small business rate to 4% by January 1, 2005. All tax rate reductions are prorated for taxation years straddling the effective dates.

(g) An Ontario surtax is levied on corporations claiming the Ontario small business deduction. This surtax "claws back" the provincial small business deduction on a graduated basis when taxable income of associated corporations falls between specified thresholds. Effective January 1, 2001, these thresholds increased from $200,000 and $500,000 to $240,000 and $600,000. The effect is to recover the entire small business deduction once the taxable income of an associated group reaches $600,000. By 2005, the lower and upper income thresholds at which the small business deduction is phased out will increase to $400,000 (lower limit) and to $1 million (upper limit).

(h) This rate will be reduced to 11% effective January 1, 2002, and to 10% effective January 1, 2003. Further proposed rate reductions will reduce the M&P rate to 8% effective January 1, 2005. This rate also applies to income derived from mining, logging, farming, or fishing activities. All tax rate reductions are prorated for taxation years straddling the effective dates.

(i) This rate will be reduced to 12.5% effective January 1, 2002, and to 11% effective January 1, 2003. Further proposed rate reductions will reduce the general rate to 8% effective January 1, 2005. All tax rate reductions are prorated for taxation years straddling the effective dates.

(j) Companies that carry on an eligible business are exempt from paying income tax for their first five taxation years. There is also a 10-year tax holiday for certain corporations that invest in major projects that give rise to significant job creation in Quebec. In addition to the above rates, there is an additional contribution to a special fund to support young persons. The rate applicable for a corporation with a December 31, 2001, year-end is 9.04%.

(k) The 16.25% rate applies to non-active business income. Including the additional special contributions noted above, the rate applicable for a corporation with a December 31, 2001, year-end is 16.51%.

(l) The New Brunswick threshold for the small business deduction increased from $200,000 to $300,000 for 2001.

(m) Certain newly incorporated small businesses are not subject to any tax on income qualifying for the small business deduction for their first three taxation years. To qualify for this exemption, certain conditions have recently been added. For example, a newly incorporated company must have at least two employees, one of whom cannot be related to a shareholder of the company.

(n) The rate for manufacturing income is 2.5% and the rate for non-manufacturing income is 6%.

Grant Thornton offices are located across Canada. We invite you to contact any of our offices directly, either through the address and phone numbers listed below, or by email. Also listed are tax contacts for each local office. You may also contact us via our Web site at **www.GrantThornton.ca**.

National Office
Royal Bank Plaza
Tenth Floor, North Tower
200 Bay Street, Box 55
Toronto, ON
M5J 2P9

Telephone: (416) 366-0100
Facsimile: (416) 360-4944
Email: National@GrantThornton.ca

Glen Gilbert, CA, IDT, Partner
National Service Line Leader, Tax
kyull@GrantThornton.ca

Karen Yull, CA, Principal
National Tax Coordinator
ggilbert@GrantThornton.ca

ANTIGONISH, N.S.
257 Main Street
P.O. Box 1480
B2G 2L7

Telephone: (902) 863-4587
Facsimile: (902) 863-0917
Email: Antigonish@GrantThornton.ca

Ben Cullen, CA, Partner
bcullen@GrantThornton.ca

BARRIE, Ont.
85 Bayfield Street
Unit 205
L4M 3A7

Telephone: (705) 730-6574
Facsimile: (705) 730-6575
Email: Barrie@GrantThornton.ca

Kirk Van Blarcom, CA, CFP, Partner
kvanblarcom@GrantThornton.ca

BATHURST, N.B.
Harbourview Place
275 Main Street
Suite 500
P.O. Box 220
E2A 3Z2

Telephone: (506) 546-6616
Facsimile: (506) 548-5622
Email: Bathurst@GrantThornton.ca

Roland Lovesey, CA,
  Office Managing Partner
rlovesey@GrantThornton.ca

BRIDGEWATER, N.S.
166 North Street
P.O. Box 220
B4V 2V6

Telephone: (902) 543-8115
Facsimile: (902) 543-7707
Email: Bridgewater@GrantThornton.ca

General Tax
Jamie Ernst, CA, Senior Manager
jernst@GrantThornton.ca

International Tax and GST/HST
Bob Oakley, CA, Office Managing Partner
roakley@GrantThornton.ca

CALGARY, Alta.
Suite 2800
500–4th Avenue SW
T2P 2V6

Telephone: (403) 260-2500
Facsimile: (403) 260-2571
Email: Calgary@GrantThornton.ca

Brian Stoddard, CA, CFP, Partner
bstoddard@GrantThornton.ca

CHARLOTTETOWN, P.E.I.
Polyclinic Professional Centre
199 Grafton Street
Suite 501
P.O. Box 187
C1A 7K4

Telephone: (902) 892-6547
Facsimile: (902) 566-5358
Email: Charlottetown@GrantThornton.ca

Paul Deighan, CA, Partner
pdeighan@GrantThornton.ca

CORNER BROOK, Nfld.
49-51 Park Street
P.O. Box 356
A2H 6E3

Telephone: (709) 634-4382
Facsimile: (709) 634-9158
Email: CornerBrook@GrantThornton.ca

Rob Flynn, CA, Partner
rflynn@GrantThornton.ca

DARTMOUTH, N.S.
Suite 301
238A Brownlow Avenue
P.O. Box 38049
B3B 1X2

Telephone: (902) 463-4900
Facsimile: (902) 469-2860
Email: Dartmouth@GrantThornton.ca

General Tax
David Blom, CA, Partner
dblom@GrantThornton.ca
Keith MacIntyre, CA, Partner
kmacintyre@GrantThornton.ca

International Tax
James Creaser, CA, Partner
jcreaser@GrantThornton.ca
GST/HST
Mark Singer, CA, Senior Manager
msinger@GrantThornton.ca

DIGBY, N.S.
Basin Place
68 Water Street
P.O. Box 848
B0V 1A0

Telephone: (902) 245-2553
Facsimile: (902) 245-6161
Email: Digby@GrantThornton.ca

General Tax
Mark Kaiser, CA, Senior Manager
mkaiser@GrantThornton.ca

International Tax and GST/HST
Bob Oakley, CA, Office Managing Partner
roakley@GrantThornton.ca

EDMONTON, Alta.
2400 Scotia Place 1
10060 Jasper Avenue NW
T5J 3R8

Telephone: (780) 422-7114
Facsimile: (780) 426-3208
Email: Edmonton@GrantThornton.ca

Terry Wainman, CA, Partner
twainman@GrantThornton.ca

General Tax and International Tax
Dan McKinley, CA, Partner
dmckinley@GrantThornton.ca

FREDERICTON, N.B.
Barker House
570 Queen Street
Suite 500
P.O. Box 1054
E3B 5C2

Telephone: (506) 458-8200
Facsimile: (506) 453-7029
Email: Fredericton@GrantThornton.ca

Patrick Cunningham, CA, Partner
pcunningham@GrantThornton.ca

GRAND FALLS–WINDSOR, Nfld.
9 High Street
P.O. Box 83
A2A 2J3

Telephone: (709) 489-6622
Facsimile: (709) 489-6625
Email: GrandFalls@GrantThornton.ca

Derrick Anthony, CA,
    Office Managing Partner
danthony@GrantThornton.ca

HALIFAX, N.S.
Cogswell Tower
2000 Barrington Street
Suite 1100
P.O. Box 426
B3J 2P8

Telephone: (902) 421-1734
Facsimile: (902) 420-1068
Email: Halifax@GrantThornton.ca

General Tax
David Blom, CA, Partner
dblom@GrantThornton.ca
John Roy, CA, Partner
jroy@GrantThornton.ca

International Tax
James Creaser, CA, Partner
jcreaser@GrantThornton.ca
GST/HST
Mark Singer, CA, Senior Manager
msinger@GrantThornton.ca

HAMILTON, Ont.
Standard Life Centre
120 King Street West
Suite 1040
L8P 4V2

Telephone: (905) 525-1930
Facsimile: (905) 527-4413
Email: Hamilton@GrantThornton.ca

General Tax
John Grummett, CA, Partner
jgrummett@GrantThornton.ca
William Kai, CA, Partner
wkai@GrantThornton.ca

GST/HST
Jean Byrnes, CA, Senior Manager
jbyrnes@GrantThornton.ca

KELOWNA, B.C.
200 – 1633 Ellis Street
V1Y 2A8

Telephone: (250) 712-6800
Facsimile: (250) 712-6850
Email: Kelowna@GrantThornton.ca

General Tax and International Tax
Jim Mills, CA, Partner
jmills@GrantThornton.ca

GST/HST
Bill Winters, CA, Partner
bwinters@GrantThornton.ca

KENTVILLE, N.S.
15 Webster Street
P.O. Box 68
B4N 3V9

Telephone: (902) 678-7307
Facsimile: (902) 679-1870
Email: Kentville@GrantThornton.ca

General Tax
Michael Van De Wiel, CA, Partner
mvandewiel@GrantThornton.ca

International Tax and GST/HST
Bob Oakley, CA, Office Managing Partner
roakley@GrantThornton.ca

LANGLEY, B.C.
Suite 200
6323 – 197th Street
V2Y 1K8

Telephone: (604) 532-3761
Facsimile: (604) 532-8130
Email: Langley@GrantThornton.ca

Don Carroll, CA, Partner
dcarroll@GrantThornton.ca

LONDON, Ont.
150 Dufferin Avenue
Suite 902
N6A 5N6

Telephone: (519) 672-2930
Facsimile: (519) 672-6455
Email: London@GrantThornton.ca

Paul Coleman, CA, CFE, Partner
paulcoleman@GrantThornton.ca

Robbie Peters, CA, Senior Manager
rpeters@GrantThornton.ca

MARKHAM, Ont.
15 Allstate Parkway
Suite 200
L3R 5B4

Telephone: (905) 475-1100
Facsimile: (905) 475-8906
Email: Markham@GrantThornton.ca

Jack Taylor, CA, Partner
jtaylor@GrantThornton.ca

MARYSTOWN, Nfld.
2 Queen Street
P.O. Box 518
A0E 2M0

Telephone: (709) 279-2300
Facsimile: (709) 279-2340
Email: Marystown@GrantThornton.ca

General Tax and GST/HST
Bill Budgell, CA, Tax Partner
bbudgell@GrantThornton.ca

General Tax and International Tax
Norman Williams, CA, CFP, Tax Partner
nwilliams@GrantThornton.ca

MIRAMICHI, N.B.
135 Henry Street
E1V 2N5

Telephone: (506) 622-0637
Facsimile: (506) 622-5174
Email: Miramichi@GrantThornton.ca

Hal Raper, CA, Office
    Managing Partner
hraper@GrantThornton.ca

MISSISSAUGA, Ont.
350 Burnhamthorpe Road West
Suite 401
L5B 3J1

Telephone: (905) 804-0905
Facsimile: (905) 804-0509
Email: Mississauga@GrantThornton.ca

General Tax
John Plestid, CA, IDT, Principal
jplestid@GrantThornton.ca

International Tax and GST/HST
Gerald Popp, CA, IDT, Office Managing Partner
gpopp@GrantThornton.ca

MONCTON, N.B.
633 Main Street
Suite 500
P.O. Box 1005
E1C 8P2

Telephone: (506) 857-0100
Facsimile: (506) 857-0105
Email: Moncton@GrantThornton.ca

General Tax
Mark Delaney, CA, Senior Manager
mdelaney@GrantThornton.ca
Kirk Ferguson, CA, Partner
kferguson@GrantThornton.ca

International Tax
Marilyn Hayre, CA, Principal
mhayre@GrantThornton.ca
General Tax and GST/HST
Steve Fowler, CA, Partner
sfowler@GrantThornton.ca

NEW GLASGOW, N.S.
Aberdeen Mall
610 East River Road
P.O. Box 427
B2H 5E5

Telephone: (902) 752-8393
Facsimile: (902) 752-4009
Email: NewGlasgow@GrantThornton.ca

Terry Kelly, CA,
    Office Managing Partner
tkelly@GrantThornton.ca

NEW LISKEARD, Ont.
17 Wellington Street
P.O. Box 2170
P0J 1P0

Telephone: (705) 647-8100
Facsimile: (705) 647-7026
Email: NewLiskeard@GrantThornton.ca

Rheo Hacquard, CA, Office
    Managing Partner
rhacquard@GrantThornton.ca

NEW WESTMINSTER, B.C.
628 Sixth Avenue
6th Floor
V3M 6Z1

Don Carroll, CA, Partner
dcarroll@GrantThornton.ca

Telephone: (604) 521-3761
Facsimile: (604) 521-8170
Email: NewWestminster@GrantThornton.ca

NORTH BAY, Ont.
222 McIntyre Street West
Suite 200
P1B 2Y8

Renzo Silveri, CA, Senior Manager
rsilveri@GrantThornton.ca

Telephone: (705) 472-6500
Facsimile: (705) 472-7760
Email: NorthBay@GrantThornton.ca

ORILLIA, Ont.
279 Coldwater Road West
L3V 3M1

David Woodman, CA,
    Office Managing Partner
dwoodman@GrantThornton.ca

Telephone: (705) 326-7605
Facsimile: (705) 326-0837
Email: Orillia@GrantThornton.ca

PEACE RIVER, Alta.
10012 – 101st Street
Box 6030
T8S 1S1

Brian Rolling, CA,
    Office Managing Partner
brolling@GrantThornton.ca

Telephone: (780) 624-3252
Facsimile: (780) 624-8758
Email: PeaceRiver@GrantThornton.ca

PORT COLBORNE, Ont.
92 Charlotte Street
Suite B
P.O. Box 336
L3K 5W1

General Tax, International Tax, GST/HST
John Grummett, CA, Partner
jgrummett@GrantThornton.ca

Telephone: (905) 834-3651
Facsimile: (905) 834-5095
Email: PortColborne@GrantThornton.ca

GST/HST
Thane MacKenzie, CA, Partner
tmackenzie@GrantThornton.ca

RICHMOND, B.C.
Suite 602, North Tower
5811 Cooney Road
V6X 3M1

General Tax
Douglas Graham, CA, Partner
dgraham@GrantThornton.ca
Doug Moore, CA, Partner
dmoore@GrantThornton.ca
Brian Tarling, CA, Partner
btarling@GrantThornton.ca
Don Carroll, CA, Partner
dcarroll@GrantThornton.ca

Telephone: (604) 278-7159
Facsimile: (604) 278-0359
Email: Richmond@GrantThornton.ca

General Tax, International Tax, GST/HST
Phil Ross, CA, Senior Manager
pross@GrantThornton.ca

SAINT JOHN, N.B.
55 Union Street
Suite 600
E2L 5B7

General Tax and International Tax
Glen Dewar, CA, Partner
gdewar@GrantThornton.ca

Telephone: (506) 634-2900
Facsimile: (506) 634-4569
Email: SaintJohn@GrantThornton.ca

GST/HST
Paul Meier, CA, Office Managing Partner
pmeier@GrantThornton.ca

SAULT STE. MARIE, Ont.
Station Tower
421 Bay Street
5th Floor
P6A 1X3

Telephone: (705) 945-9700
Facsimile: (705) 945-9705
Email: SaultSteMarie@GrantThornton.ca

Barry Magill, CA,
   Office Managing Partner
bmagill@GrantThornton.ca

Stephen Hussey, CA, CIP, CA (SA) Partner
shussey@GrantThornton.ca

ST. CATHARINES, Ont.
55 King Street
Suite 304
P.O. Box 2011
L2R 7R7

Telephone: (905) 688-4822
Facsimile: (905) 688-4837
Email: StCatharines@GrantThornton.ca

John Grummett, CA, Partner
jgrummett@GrantThornton.ca

ST. JOHN'S, Nfld.
ICON Building
187 Kenmount Road
P.O. Box 8037
A1B 3M7

Telephone: (709) 722-5960
Facsimile: (709) 722-7892
Email: StJohns@GrantThornton.ca

General Tax and GST/HST
Bill Budgell, CA, Tax Partner
bbudgell@GrantThornton.ca

General Tax and International Tax
Norman Williams, CA, CFP, Tax Partner
nwilliams@GrantThornton.ca

SUMMERSIDE, P.E.I.
Royal Bank Building
220 Water Street
P.O. Box 1660
C1N 2V5

Telephone: (902) 436-9155
Facsimile: (902) 436-6913
Email: Summerside@GrantThornton.ca

Byron Murray, CA, Office Managing Partner
bmurray@GrantThornton.ca

SYDNEY, N.S.
Suite 200, George Place
500 George Street
B1P 1K6

Telephone: (902) 562-5581
Facsimile: (902) 562-0073
Email: Sydney@GrantThornton.ca

Patrick Lahey, CA, Manager
plahey@GrantThornton.ca

TORONTO, Ont.
Royal Bank Plaza
19th Floor, South Tower
200 Bay Street
P.O. Box 55
M5J 2P9

Telephone: (416) 366-0100
Facsimile: (416) 360-4949
Email: Toronto@GrantThornton.ca

General Tax
Glen Gilbert, CA, IDT, Partner
ggilbert@GrantThornton.ca

GST/HST
Cathy Kuhrt, CA, IDT, Partner
ckuhrt@GrantThornton.ca
International Tax
Gary Dent, CA, Partner
gdent@GrantThornton.ca

TRURO, N.S.
Bank of Montreal Building
35 Commercial Street
Suite 400
P.O. Box 725
B2N 5E8

Telephone: (902) 893-1150
Facsimile: (902) 893-9757
Email: Truro@GrantThornton.ca

Gerry Hutchings, CA, CHRP,
   Office Managing Partner
ghutchings@GrantThornton.ca

VANCOUVER, B.C.
Royal Centre
1055 West Georgia Street
Suite 2800
P.O. Box 11177
V6E 4N3

Telephone: (604) 687-2711
Facsimile: (604) 685-6569
Email: Vancouver@GrantThornton.ca

General Tax
Douglas Graham, CA, Partner
dgraham@GrantThornton.ca
Doug Moore, CA, Partner
dmoore@GrantThornton.ca

General Tax and International Tax
Brian Tarling, CA, Partner
btarling@GrantThornton.ca
General Tax and GST/HST
Don Carroll, CA, Partner
dcarroll@GrantThornton.ca

VICTORIA, B.C.
888 Fort Street
Third Floor
V8W 1H8

Telephone: (250) 383-4191
Facsimile: (250) 381-4623
Email: Victoria@GrantThornton.ca

General Tax and International Tax
Susan Mehinagic, CA, LLB, Partner
smehinagic@GrantThornton.ca

GST/HST
Peter Lloyd, CA, CIP, Office Managing Partner
plloyd@GrantThornton.ca
Joyce Gillen, CA, Senior Manager
jgillen@GrantThornton.ca

WETASKIWIN, Alta.
5108 – 51st Avenue
T9A 0V2

Telephone: (780) 352-1679
Facsimile: (780) 352-2451
Email: Wetaskiwin@GrantThornton.ca

Tony Estabrooks, CA, Partner
testabrooks@GrantThornton.ca

WINNIPEG, Man.
900–One Lombard Place
R3B 0X3

Telephone: (204) 944-0100
Facsimile: (204) 957-5442
Email: Winnipeg@GrantThornton.ca

John Granelli, CA, CFP, Partner
jgranelli@GrantThornton.ca

YARMOUTH, N.S.
328 Main Street
P.O. Box 297
B5A 4B2

Telephone: (902) 742-7842
Facsimile: (902) 742-0224
Email: Yarmouth@GrantThornton.ca

General Tax
Martin Rutherford, CA, Partner
mrutherford@GrantThornton.ca

International Tax and GST/HST
Bob Oakley, CA, Office Managing Partner
roakley@GrantThornton.ca

Grant Thornton practices as Raymond Chabot Grant Thornton in Quebec:
Montreal (514) 878-2691
Ottawa (613) 563-0210

Active business: An "active business" includes any business, as well as an adventure or concern in the nature of trade, except (i) a business that derives its income from property (including interest, dividends, royalties, and rent) and has fewer than six full-time employees; and (ii) a business that provides personal services through a corporation that has fewer than six full-time employees and where the individuals providing the services would be considered employees or officers of the entity using those services, were it not for the presence of the corporation.

Active business income: "Active business income" uses corporate income as the benchmark for calculating certain tax credits. It includes income derived from an active business (including incidental income from its active business, such as interest earned on customers' delinquent receivables) and specifically excludes income derived from property, such as capital gains, interest, dividends, royalties, and rent.

Annuity: An "annuity" is a form of investment that yields a sequence of periodic payments, usually equal, at equivalent intervals of time (e.g., $1,200 every month). In return for a single payment to the provider, the annuitant receives a series of payments for a specific term that can begin immediately or be deferred. Annuities can have a variety of options associated with them.

Arm's length: At "arm's length" indicates that the parties to a transaction are unrelated and have separate interests for entering the transaction. A "non-arm's-length" transaction would be one between related parties or between parties with a common interest acting in concert.

Calendar year: A "calendar year" occurs between January 1 and December 31.

Capital asset: A "capital asset" is one a business intends to use in its daily operations for the production or supply of goods and services, for rental to others, or for administrative purposes and is not intended for sale in the ordinary course of business (such as an inventory item). A depreciable asset is an example of a capital asset.

Carry-forward: A "carry-forward" arises when a loss or tax credit is not fully used in the current period and, as a result, the unused portion may be used in the future. For example, a loss carry-forward arises when a taxpayer has incurred a loss in the current period and cannot use it to offset income from a previous period. The loss can be carried forward to offset future income.

Common-law partner: A person of the opposite sex or same sex who cohabited with you and who either cohabited with you for at least one year in a conjugal relationship or is the parent of your child. This definition applies for 2001 and subsequent years.

Depreciation: "Depreciation" is an accounting procedure that aims at distributing the cost of tangible capital assets, less any expected salvage value, over the estimated useful life of the asset, in a rational and systematic manner. The depreciation is the portion of the total cost allocated to a given period.

Fair market value: "Fair market value" reflects the highest price that can be obtained for an asset between informed parties who deal at arm's length and are under no compulsion to act.

Fiscal year-end: The "fiscal year-end" for a business is the point in time it has chosen to account for its profits and losses. Generally, a corporation may choose any date in the year, but special rules exist for individuals and partnerships (see article 2). Once a business establishes the date for its fiscal year-end, it cannot be changed for tax purposes without the CCRA's approval.

Flow-through share: A "flow-through share" is a form of investment related specifically to the resource industry. Unlike a typical share, certain expenditures incurred by the corporation can be renounced by the corporation and "flowed through" to the shareholders. The shareholders can then deduct these items on their own tax returns.

Goodwill: "Goodwill" is an intangible asset that represents the superior earning power of a business. Generally, the value assigned to the goodwill of a business is the fair market value of the business as a whole, less the fair market value of the net tangible assets and identifiable intangible assets that constitute the business.

Holding company: A "holding company" is a corporation whose principal purpose is to hold investment assets such as shares in other companies and portfolio investments.

Information returns: "Information returns" are forms or documents containing tax-related information about individuals, corporations, trusts, or other entities that must be filed for the CCRA to administer the provisions of the Income Tax Act.

Joint venture: A "joint venture" results from a contractual arrangement whereby two or more entities jointly control an economic activity. Unlike other investments, none of the entities can exercise unilateral control over the joint venture, regardless of the ownership interest. A joint venture has no legal status in itself. The venturers may own property in common, but each has a direct share in the property.

Limited partnership: In a "limited partnership," the partners have limited liability. As with shareholders of a corporation, liability is restricted to the amount invested. There must be at least one general partner who is fully liable for the debts of the partnership, while the general and limited partners share the partnership's profits in accordance with the terms of the agreement.

Marginal tax rate: "Marginal tax rates" are the income tax rates that apply to each dollar of additional income at different levels of taxable income. As an individual's income level rises, his or her marginal tax rate also rises.

Non-refundable tax credit: A "non-refundable tax credit" is one that is applied to reduce income tax payable for a given year but is limited to reducing taxes to nil. If a portion of the tax credit remains unused after reducing taxes to nil, it cannot be used to create a refund. The basic personal credit is an example of a non-refundable tax credit.

Partnership: A "partnership" is an arrangement between persons carrying on a business in common to earn a profit. It can be formed by a group of individuals, corporations, or a combination, thereof. The partners share the net profits and not the gross returns of a business. A partnership can be formed by verbal or written agreement and is governed by provincial law.

Recapture: A "recapture" is an income item created when the balance of the undepreciated capital cost (UCC) of a class of depreciable assets becomes negative. This can occur when the proceeds of disposition of a capital asset (which is limited to the original cost of the asset) is applied to reduce the UCC of the class and results in a negative balance. In essence, capital cost allowance (CCA) had been recorded in excess of the asset's remaining economic value. On the sale of the assets of that class, a portion of the previous CCA is recovered.

Renunciation: "Renunciation" is the process of forgoing, or giving up, a particular benefit in a formal manner. Certain tax credits or deductions can be renounced in favour of an alternative treatment.

Reserve: A "reserve" is generally an income amount that relates to a future period and can therefore be set aside and included then. A reserve is excluded from the current period's income and included in the next one. A new reserve would be established in the next period if applicable.

Retained earnings: "Retained earnings" is a term used to describe the total net after-tax income of a corporation, less distributions of dividends to shareholders that have accumulated since incorporation.

Share capital: Basically, "share capital" is the owners' investment in a corporation, represented by common and preferred shares. A monetary value is assigned to shares when they are first issued from the treasury of a corporation.

Spouse: A person of the opposite sex to whom you are legally married. This definition applies for 2001 and subsequent years.

Superannuation: "Superannuation" is synonymous with a pension benefit and includes any amount received out of a pension fund or plan. Some examples of a superannuation would be Old Age Security payments, Canada Pension Plan payments, and payments from a privately established pension plan.

Testamentary trust: A "testamentary trust" is one created as a consequence of an individual's death.

Writeoff: A "writeoff" is a deduction used to reduce net income for tax purposes.

Index

Keep up with ever-changing tax regulations and rates year round

Visit our Web site at **www.GrantThornton.ca/tax** and sign up for Smart Tax Tips online. Approximately every two weeks, you'll receive notification by email of the current Smart Tax Tip posted on our Web site. And, for the most up-to-date information on federal tax credits, federal and provincial personal tax rates, corporate tax rates, and employment insurance rates, you'll also find continually updated tax tables.

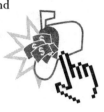

More for you on our Web site ...

- Explore a wide variety of topics important to business owners, including tax strategies, strategic and financing issues—access Grant Thornton management issues papers at **www.GrantThornton.ca/resources**.
- Learn how some business owners found solutions to difficult issues by accessing our case studies at **www.GrantThornton.ca/resources**.
- Find new business opportunities or capitalize on the value in your own business—check out our Business Buy and Sell e-tool at **www.GrantThornton.ca/buyandsell**.
- Find out what other business owners across Canada think about e-commerce and the top issues they face as they run their businesses—read our survey results at **www.GrantThornton.ca/resources**.
- Individuals can find out how to save taxes, create a family trust, and much more by accessing our management issues papers for individuals at **www.GrantThornton.ca/resources**.

With our compliments …

Send now for your complimentary subscription to *Cataly$t*, the Grant Thornton newsletter focusing on business issues facing entrepreneurial businesses, owner-managers, and not-for-profit organizations.

Fax this form to:

Cataly$t

Grant Thornton LLP

Chartered Accountants/

Management Consultants

Fax: (416) 360-4944

Name: _____

Title: _____

Company: _____

Business Mailing Address: _____

_____

City: _____ Prov.: _____

Postal Code: _____

Business phone: (_____) _____ - _____

Business fax: (_____) _____ - _____

Email: _____

Type of business:

__ Private Corporation

__ Public Corporation

__ Proprietorship

__ Partnership

__ Limited Partnership

__ Joint Venture

__ Professional Practice

Ownership:

__ Owner-managed

__ Not owner-managed

__ Not-for-profit

Business description: _____

Check the most appropriate:

__ Agriculture and Fisheries

__ Business Services

__ Communications

__ Construction

__ Finance and Real Estate

__ Government

__ Health Care

__ High-technology Industries

__ Hospitality and Entertainment

__ Manufacturing and Distribution

__ Not-for-profit

__ Professional Services

__ Resource Industries

__ Transportation

__ Wholesale and Retail Trade

Number of employees: _____

Annual sales volume: _____